T0265957

Emotional
Sobriety II

The Next Frontier

Books Published by AA Grapevine, Inc.

The Language of the Heart (& eBook)

The Best of the Grapevine Volume I (eBook only)

The Best of Bill (& eBook)

Thank You for Sharing

I Am Responsible: The Hand of AA

The Home Group: Heartbeat of AA (& eBook)

Emotional Sobriety I & II— (& eBook)

Spiritual Awakenings I & II (& eBook)

In Our Own Words: Stories of Young AAs in Recovery (& eBook)

Beginners' Book (& eBook)

Voices of Long-Term Sobriety (& eBook)

A Rabbit Walks Into A Bar

Step by Step — Real AAs, Real Recovery (& eBook)

Young & Sober (& eBook)

Into Action (& eBook)

Happy, Joyous & Free (& eBook)

One on One (& eBook)

No Matter What (& eBook)

Grapevine Daily Quote Book (& eBook)

Sober & Out (& eBook)

Forming True Partnerships (& eBook)

Our Twelve Traditions (& eBook)

Making Amends (& eBook)

Voices of Women in AA (& eBook)

AA in the Military (& eBook)

One Big Tent (& eBook)

Take me to your Sponsor (& eBook)

IN SPANISH

El lenguaje del corazón

Lo mejor de Bill (& eBook)

El grupo base: Corazón de AA

Lo mejor de La Viña

Felices, alegres y libres (& eBook)

Un día a la vez (& eBook)

Frente A Frente (& eBook)

Bajo El Mismo Techo (& eBook)

IN FRENCH

Le langage du coeur

Les meilleurs articles de Bill

Le Groupe d'attache: Le battement du coeur des AA

En tête à tête (& eBook)

Heureux, joyeux et libres (& eBook)

La sobriété émotive

Emotional Sobriety II

The Next Frontier

AAGRAPEVINE, Inc.
New York, New York
www.aagrapevine.org

Sixth printing 2024

AA Preamble

Alcoholics Anonymous is a fellowship of people
who share their experience, strength and hope
with each other that they may solve their common problem
and help others to recover from alcoholism.

The only requirement for membership is a desire to stop drinking.
There are no dues or fees for AA membership;
we are self-supporting through our own contributions.
AA is not allied with any sect, denomination, politics, organization
or institution; does not wish to engage in any controversy,
neither endorses nor opposes any causes.

Our primary purpose is to stay sober
and help other alcoholics to achieve sobriety.

©AA Grapevine, Inc.

Contents

SECTION FOUR
More Will Be Revealed

SECTION FIVE
Rooms of Our Own

SECTION SIX
Steps to Serenity

SECTION SEVEN
Finding Our Inner Adult

The Next Frontier— Emotional Sobriety

think that many oldsters who have put our AA "booze cure" to severe but successful tests still find they often lack emotional sobriety. Perhaps they will be the spearhead for the next major development in AA—the development of much more real maturity and balance (which is to say, humility) in our relations with ourselves, with our fellows, and with God.

Those adolescent urges that so many of us have for top approval, perfect security, and perfect romance—urges quite appropriate to age seventeen—prove to be an impossible way of life when we are at age forty-seven or fifty-seven.

Since AA began, I've taken immense wallops in all these areas because of my failure to grow up, emotionally and spiritually. My God, how painful it is to keep demanding the impossible, and how very painful to discover finally, that all along we have had the cart before the horse! Then comes the final agony of seeing how awfully wrong we have been, but still finding ourselves unable to get off the emotional merry-go-round.

How to translate a right mental conviction into a right emotional result, and so into easy, happy and good living—well, that's not only the neurotic's problem, it's the problem of life itself for all of us who have got to the point of real willingness to hew to right principles in all our affairs.

Even then, as we hew away, peace and joy may still elude us. That's the place so many of us AA oldsters have come to. And it's a hell of a spot, literally. How shall our unconscious—from which so many of our fears, compulsions and phony aspirations still stream—be brought into line with what we actually believe, know and want! How to convince our dumb, raging and hidden "Mr. Hyde" becomes our main task.

I've recently come to believe that this can be achieved. I believe so because I begin to see many benighted ones—folks like you and me—commencing to get results. Last autumn [several years back—ed.], depression, having no really rational cause at all, almost took me to the cleaners. I began to be scared that I was in for another long chronic spell. Considering the grief I've had with depressions, it wasn't a bright prospect.

I kept asking myself, "Why can't the Twelve Steps work to release depression?" By the hour, I stared at the St. Francis Prayer ... "It's better to comfort than to be comforted." Here was the formula, all right. But why didn't it work?

Suddenly I realized what the matter was. My basic flaw had always been dependence—almost absolute dependence—on people or circumstances to supply me with prestige, security, and the like. Failing to get these things according to my perfectionist dreams and specifications, I had fought for them. And when defeat came, so did my depression.

There wasn't a chance of making the outgoing love of St. Francis a workable and joyous way of life until these fatal and almost absolute dependencies were cut away.

Because I had over the years undergone a little spiritual development, the absolute quality of these frightful dependencies had never before been so starkly revealed. Reinforced by what Grace I could secure in prayer, I found I had to exert every ounce of will and action to cut off these faulty emotional dependencies upon people, upon AA, indeed, upon any set of circumstances whatsoever.

Then only could I be free to love as Francis had. Emotional and instinctual satisfactions, I saw, were really the extra dividends of having love, offering love, and expressing, a love appropriate to each relation of life.

Plainly, I could not avail myself of God's love until I was able to offer it back to Him by loving others as He would have me. And I couldn't possibly do that so long as I was victimized by false dependencies.

For my dependency meant demand—a demand for the possession and control of the people and the conditions surrounding me.

While those words "absolute dependency" may look like a gimmick, they were the ones that helped to trigger my release into my present degree of stability and quietness of mind, qualities which I am now trying to consolidate by offering love to others regardless of the return to me.

This seems to be the primary healing circuit: an outgoing love of God's creation and His people, by means of which we avail ourselves of His love for us. It is most clear that the real current can't flow until our paralyzing dependencies are broken, and broken at depth. Only then can we possibly have a glimmer of what adult love really is.

Spiritual calculus, you say? Not a bit of it. Watch any AA of six months working with a new Twelfth Step case. If the case says "To the devil with you" the Twelfth Stepper only smiles and turns to another case. He doesn't feel frustrated or rejected. If his next case responds, and in turn starts to give love and attention to other alcoholics, yet gives none back to him, the sponsor is happy about it anyway. He still doesn't feel rejected; instead he rejoices that his one-time prospect is sober and happy. And if his next following case turns out in later time to be his best friend (or romance) then the sponsor is most joyful. But he well knows that his happiness is a by-product—the extra dividend of giving without any demand for a return.

The really stabilizing thing for him was having and offering love to that strange drunk on his doorstep. That was Francis at work, powerful and practical, minus dependency and minus demand.

In the first six months of my own sobriety, I worked hard with many alcoholics. Not a one responded. Yet this work kept me sober. It wasn't a question of those alcoholics giving me anything. My stability came out of trying to give, not out of demanding that I receive.

Thus I think it can work out with emotional sobriety. If we examine every disturbance we have, great or small, we will find at the root of it some unhealthy dependency and its consequent unhealthy demand. Let us, with God's help, continually surrender these hobbling demands. Then we can be set free to live and love; we may then be able to Twelfth Step ourselves and others into emotional sobriety.

Of course I haven't offered you a really new idea—only a gimmick that has started to unhook several of my own "hexes" at depth. Nowadays my brain no longer races compulsively in either elation, grandiosity or depression. I have been given a quiet place in bright sunshine.

Bill W.

SECTION ONE

The Great Balancing Act

Though balance is one of the most underrated attributes of all, being non-dramatic and low-key, we observe that the label "unbalanced," applied to a person, is never a desired one. Balance is one of the gifts of long-term sobriety that seem to be appreciated later or, by the unusually mature, at any time.

From San José, a member describes balance to a "T" in 1976, after noting the faux ecstasies of his drinking days. "Today, by the grace of God, I strive for a basically bland diet. For example, on this day I've worked eight hours, washed my clothes, gone to a meeting, and written a poem about gratitude. Later, I'll meditate. Dull by my past standards, but pleasantly sane by my AA way of thinking."

Before he discovered Step Eleven and meditation, Ken of Ames, Iowa, writes that he was powerless over unhappiness and his life was unmanageable. "Long before I was a binge drinker," he adds, "I was a binge thinker. I tended to think incessantly." His mind had no "off" switch, coming up with grudges, resentments, and so on, creating the state of imbalance, ripe for relapse.

When Jim of Largo, Florida's home group holds a workshop on emotional sobriety, he becomes convinced that time in the program is not enough to ensure it, and that certain emotions will remain deadly because they "block me from dealing in a mature, emotionally sober way, rather than just reacting."

With his new sense of balance, Bruce H. of Arlington, Virginia, decides he doesn't have to memorize anything in the Big Book after all; neither does he have to arrange the chairs perfectly every time. And G.P. of Elbert, Colorado admits that when the pink cloud hit him, "I went insane. Quite starkly mad. ... For one thing, I couldn't say no—a clear indication of insanity. ... I accepted five full-time job offers, and was thinking of a sixth." He also bought everything in sight.

Newly sober; deeply imbalanced.

"Thank the Higher Power," he writes. "The malady doesn't seem to be permanent."

By Our Attitudes

January 1950

A little clock in a jeweler's window stopped one morning at 20 minutes past 8. School children, noticing the time, stopped to play. People on their way to the train stopped to chat a little longer and all were late because one little clock had stopped. Never had these people realized how much they had depended on that clock in the jeweler's window until the day it failed them and led them all astray.

We AAs are very much like that clock. Day after day there are those who are looking to us for guidance and direction on the way of life. If our AA life is functioning properly, we are faithful guides to all who observe us. But if something has gone wrong with our AA way of life, we are stopped clocks, and unfortunate indeed is the man who permits himself to be misled by our example. We who have been helped by AA are as letters of God addressed to our friends and fellow men. By our attitudes, our speech, and our behavior are we to show them the transforming power of AA's philosophy of life.

C.T.
St. Paul, Minnesota

The Golden Mean

(from PO Box 1980) November 1976

In my drinking days, excitement was measured by the degree of my emotions. My ecstasy came from the fleeting highs of alcohol and sex and from the appealing but dangerous depths of writings about suicide. The in-between—moderation—was despised as a malady of the "common folk."

Today, by the grace of God, I strive for a basically bland diet. For example, on this day I've worked eight hours, washed my clothes, gone to a meeting, and written a poem about gratitude. Later, I'll meditate. Dull by my past standards, but pleasantly sane by my AA way of thinking.

Bob P.
San José, California

Binge Thinker
July 2010

Before I was powerless over alcohol and my life had become unmanageable, I was powerless over unhappiness and my life had become unmanageable. I turned to alcohol in my late 40s as the best self-help option I thought I could find. Often, my unhappiness seemed to melt as I drank. But drinking became an ever more elusive and flawed solution to my unhappiness. It began to create unhappiness of its own. My overall unhappiness was eventually much greater than what I had evaded and yet not solved at the beginning of my alcoholism. Now what?

Maybe the best way to feel was to be happy. How was that possible?

Long before I was a binge drinker, I was a binge thinker. I tended to think incessantly, as if this were an essential part of staying alive. My mind either had no "off" switch, or, if it did, I had no idea where it was. In this constant banter, I could find all sorts of resentments to chew on, grudges to hold, victimization to ponder and catastrophes to protest. Life was unfair, people were the harbingers of much injustice and unkindness, and I was justifiably withholding my seal of approval by not accepting what already was.

I create thoughts. I can do so from default behaviors (what I have come to otherwise recognize as "character defects"), or I can create thoughts within the awareness of having choices. Awareness for me is realizing that I am not my thoughts. Rather, I observe my thoughts and their creation and content. If I need not be run by my conditioned default thinking, then have I discovered the choice of observing and creating constructive thinking?

Once I learned to meditate, as encouraged in Step Eleven, I was able to find the "off" switch to my thinking when that thinking is neither needed nor useful to me. I can use thought, rather than have my thinking use me. "Awareness," I believe, is the most accessible doorway to what has been referred to as "spirituality" throughout my life and in AA.

Ken T.
Ames, Iowa

It's Not the Shoelace
May 2010

Recently, my home group conducted a workshop exploring emotional sobriety. We broke it up into different aspects such as "What is emotional sobriety?", "How does it differ from physical sobriety?", etc. My assignment was to explore why we need emotional sobriety and I presented it as follows:

When I first came to AA my emotions rose to the surface, where I became aware of them. While I thought that I had successfully submerged them with alcohol when I was drinking, I can't deny that I often drank at "him," "her," "Mom," "Dad," the boss, some unfair customer, a disrespectful sales clerk, the police, the system, or whatever. I could say that alcohol let me not feel, but the truth is that I felt everything and often wanted to show "them."

I used drinking to hurt others or plot my revenge. The only blessing was that I often wouldn't even remember the plot when I sobered up. Newly sober, I not only had the feelings but I also had a lack of ability to deal with them. My immaturity came out in full force. My old idea was that alcohol would still work with these feelings, and I would sometimes give in. Even if I didn't drink, I could be miserable and hold grudges. That's when something trivial like a broken shoelace might lead me to drink because it was the last straw.

Without the help of God and a sponsor, I might never know that it wasn't the shoelace but the lingering grudge and my lack of emotional sobriety that led to drinking again. While this lack of emotional sobriety was dangerous when I was newly sober, the danger did not go away just because I've achieved some time in AA. Indeed, I can mistake number of years for a degree of emotional sobriety. I can rest on my laurels without even recognizing it.

When I hold on to resentments, when I find things unforgivable, when I am jealous of another's success, when I am unwilling to listen to others and change my mind, when I react severely to criticism even as I congratulate myself for another day or month or year of not drinking, I am not only not emotionally sober, but I also may become not physically sober. This can happen even if I once had a spiritual awakening and have many years of sobriety behind me. The Tenth Step tells me to "watch for selfishness, dishonesty, resentment, and fear" not because these emotions are so deadly in themselves, but because they block me from dealing in a mature, emotionally sober way, rather than just reacting. Since the essay on the Step next says, "and when they crop up," it is a sure bet that time in the program will not make me immune from these negative emotions and my ensuing reactions. My reactions can include drinking again, but even if I don't drink, I can cause problems and heartache in the lives of those who love me and work with me.

As the book says, "We believe a man who says sobriety is enough is unthinking." For the sake of others if not for myself, I should seek emotional sobriety.

When I am letting myself be ruled by "selfishness, dishonesty, resentment, and fear," any rational thinking or action I do would be purely by accident. Likewise, serenity would be elusive at best and non-existent at worst. As a friend says, my biggest job in a spiritual life is to become undisturbed. I would only have one of two reactions to any negative interaction with another person: I would either forgive the other person or make amends.

I have made a real advance in emotional sobriety if I finally realize I do not have to react to a slight by striking back.

Finally, I was told to live a day at a time but not told how to do that. I submit that it is impossible to do a day at a time when bedeviled by emotional chaos. If I strive for emotional sobriety, I will have a much better chance of living in the now, which can lead to joy and appreciation for the wonder of my life.

Jim H.
Largo, Florida

Carrying the Message
February 1971

After six years of sobriety, I recently went through my first really long (four weeks) depression. Doctors had given me some bad news about my eyes, and I immediately exaggerated their diagnosis. I went around telling myself I had to accept blindness and, "Thank God I would not be a drunken blind man." I thought I was applying the Eleventh Step (to the best of my ability), but I could see it was not working, and I proceeded into a very bad depression. I used all the gimmicks I was taught in AA—except "Let Go and Let God" and "One Day at a Time"—but nothing was working.

Then I met a doctor who told me things were not as bad as I thought—it seems I was hearing only what I wanted to hear. However, the depression continued. Along about this time, I had some difficulty with someone I was sponsoring, and the result was another emotional upheaval, which did not help the situation.

I began talking to good friends and members of my group, and things started to look a little better. I found my "conscious contact" through these friends. I found that "Let Go and Let God" does work and, most important of all, that "One Day at a Time" was something

I had to apply. I also attended many meetings. I have to be honest
and say I did think about drinking, but thank God I did not drink.
I put myself through the meat grinder on this emotional binge—
self-condemnation, doubts, etc.—but I think it was for a reason.
I think I have greater understanding for someone going through
these things, and I also learned to love the person who has been
slipping around and coming back. Have I ever experienced such humility and willingness as that poor soul? I am feeling much better
now, and I thank God for AA and my good friends. I have learned
how to accept their help.

J.P.K.
Queens, New York

Chair Master

October 1997

Those first few weeks in AA, Frank had begun to drive me nuts.
He couldn't resist. At the end of every meeting, as soon as
I left the table and headed toward the door, he would yell
across the room, "Hey, Bruce!" I would stop, turn, and wait for
it. Grinning ear to ear, he would give me the wink and pointed fin-
ger and say, "Be good to yourself!" I would nod and mumble, "Sure,
Frank, sure," and go to the car.

Driving, I would begin the internal dialogue: What the heck does
that mean? Be good to myself? I was good to myself—that's what got
me into church basements trying not to drink a day at a time, trying
to understand the meaning of AA, trying to relate to guys like Frank.
I'd been too good to myself—rewarding myself with booze, giving myself a break with booze, cozying into the bottle in the basement—and
look where it got me. I figured I needed to do the opposite of being
good to myself. I need to get tough with myself: stop this stuff that I
obviously couldn't handle. How did Frank get sober and stay sober all
these years, if that's his philosophy, and why the devil is he singling

me out with that dopey farewell after every meeting?

But I liked Frank. There was something about him. He was a rugged, confident, good-looking guy in his forties, with a toughness about him, a directness in his approach to the AA program. He had years of sobriety and when he talked, gesturing in a relaxed way, he reminded the group frequently that his father was Italian and his father always said don't worry about it, it will always work out, and he would add, "And it all will, a day at a time, if I don't take a drink and give it a chance." When Frank talked, the others around the table smiled and nodded and gave him respect. I did too—and he seemed to like me and listened to me when I talked. Then he gave that parting shot as I was leaving!

I'm a doer. Always was. I was brought up that way. My mother told me, "You're the best; you can do anything anybody else can; set your goal; follow your star." My dad said, "Don't be lazy; get to work; I've got a job for you."

I was a doer when drinking, too. I drank through college and finished with honors (never mind the hospitalization for ulcers senior year and the medical caution about drinking). I drank through a marriage and held it together for sixteen years (it wasn't the drinking that caused the divorce, it was that incompatibility thing). I drank through three good jobs and always moved up, got promotions, made more money. (Okay, maybe the problem I had with those martinis in the last job was beginning to show a little, but I was never arrested, was I?)

Sobering up in the group with Frank and the others, I was still a doer. I ran at AA like I was running to the arms of my mother, eager to show that I was the best, ready for the compliment. I got to the church early, set up the chairs, learned (from an old guy named John) the special technique of making coffee in not one but two big pots (I'll make the best coffee, they'll taste the improvement), and on my six-month anniversary I was asked to be Friday night program chairman. Terrific, I thought, they recognize my leadership ability. I'll do the best job yet.

And I did. The Friday night programs got more interesting. I found different ways to bring everybody out, get them to speak. I passed around the "Twelve and Twelve," got people to read in turn. The group hadn't done that before. They thought it was neat. I photocopied sections of the Big Book and the Hazelden guide to get folks into the Fourth and Fifth Steps. People were responding. I felt good, proud even.

Frank kept saying, "Hey, Bruce, be good to yourself!" And I kept trying not to be annoyed. But now there was a slightly sterner tone in Frank's voice. The smile was there, but he was serious.

After I'd been sober in the group for a year, I had moved from coffee maker to chairperson to program chairperson to chairperson of the group. I didn't know that groups had chairpeople. I had been to some that didn't, but mine did and when I found out there was a leadership ladder, I was in my element. Set your goal, son. I did, in AA as out there, and here I was, at the top of this group. And I was secretly memorizing not only all the Steps but chapter five in the Big Book and key passages from the "Twelve and Twelve." I wondered if anybody had ever been able to recite, in perfect order, the names of the people whose stories were in the Big Book. That would be impressive! I resolved to do it.

Then it began to hit the fan. One Friday night an older woman named Maude couldn't read the photocopied sheet I had handed out because she had left her glasses home, and before I could show my flexibility and initiative by switching to another format or reading it for her, the next guy said, "Why don't we forget this reading stuff and just talk about it?" And before I could smile and accept this, the next guy and the one across the table were shoving their sheets into the middle of the table and growling a little. Shambles. And then John said that the woman who was making the coffee had quit showing up and what was I going to do about it. And a week after that, a small delegation, all old-timers, pulled me aside after the meeting and said (I forget the exact words, because I was so steamed): "Too much is changing. People aren't used to it. Maybe it's time for you to give somebody else a turn."

Two hours later, Frank found me. Corner table, neighborhood bar. Drinking soda. Thinking. Tired. Thinking. Lonely. Thinking. Angry. I told him, as he settled into the other chair, a little smile on his face, a nonchalant order to the waitress for "what he's having," that I was totally demoralized.

"What do you think the problem is?"

"I don't know. I was trying my best. I thought I was doing a good job, but Tom and Suzy said—"

He raised his hands. "Whoa. Tell me that part about trying your best."

"Just that. I tried damned hard to give something to the group, to make it better, if I could."

"You think that could be the problem?"

"I upset the group by really getting involved?"

"Right now I don't care about the group. I'm looking at you."

"You see a guy that's about ready to give up."

Frank took a leisurely drink of his soda and wiped the corners of his mouth with the back of his hand. He looked me in the eye and I looked away, down into the glass in front of me. But I was all ears. Frank was talking: "You know what being good to yourself means? In your case, I think it means don't try so hard. Getting sober is not some contest you have to win. You're not being good to yourself by putting yourself into a stressful situation. And AA sure is not the place for stress. It's just the opposite."

It's been more than twenty years since I left that bar with Frank, and my understanding of AA and what it means to me has grown from that moment. "Easy Does It" is not something that comes naturally to me. But within AA, it has come to make sense. Since that shaky beginning and the talk that night with Frank, I've found my place in the Fellowship. It is not up front, trying to be in charge. I try to contribute when it's my turn; I lead a meeting when asked; if chairs need setting up, I do it for fun and not as Chair Master. Relaxing in the program, in Frank's philosophy, and not trying too hard have become the gift of daily sobriety and a new way of life. Every day, every meeting, there's something more to learn. I am sober. I am being good to myself.

And occasionally I will spot him—the guy who is so uptight, the guy who is beating himself up because he's not perfect, the guy who is trying so damned hard to get it right—and I'll meet him for coffee or talk to him after the meeting. I'm not Frank; I can't say to him, in front of the group, "Be good to yourself!" But I'll tell him my story, and how I came to understand that trying too hard in AA isn't good for me. Sometimes the guy will say that it makes sense to him, too.

Bruce H.
Arlington, Virginia

Honeymoon

January 1975

A nybody who grabs the program and makes it past the end of the physical hassles—the shock when your liver finally realizes it's got a new shot at life and starts functioning normally again, when your digestive system starts to see food again, real food, and not that strange chemical that kept putting it out of whack—anybody who makes it that far enters what many repaired drunks ("recovered" sounds so medical) call the AA honeymoon. It's that wonderful period, lasting from ninety days on up, when life is so damn fine, when everything works so ... so right, somehow, that it's hard to believe you're just returning to normal and not becoming some kind of superman.

The honeymoon strikes people differently, depending on individual traits, depth of addiction, withdrawal problems, and the like. Some become ebullient, bubbling with smiles and joy; others walk around in a seemingly permanent state of euphoria or shock; still others can't believe the feeling and seem stunned. (A good friend who caught the stick the program offers told me, "Do you know, really know, what it's like to suddenly be able to tie your shoes with both eyes open?")

I went insane. Quite starkly mad. Perhaps not clinically (although everybody in the program seems to know all about psychological terms and what they really mean), but if outward actions are any indication, I was ready for the men in white coats and the quiet, screened rooms.

For one thing, I couldn't say no—a clear indication of insanity. At one point, when I'd been dry about six weeks, I had accepted five full-time job offers and was seriously considering the sixth when my wife ran screaming from the house—babbling something about my blank eyes and wide smile—to get my sponsor and save me from myself. I firmly believed I could actually do all five jobs at the same time. Worse, I accepted invitations to four parties—all on the same night. And we made all four, too, though it took my wife nine Al-Anon meetings before she mastered the twitching. She still, though I've been dry over a year now, automatically says no to everything.

On top of my inability to say no, or perhaps coupled with it, was the seemingly automatic compulsion to buy things. Anything. If I wanted it, I'd buy it, completely on impulse. I now own and will probably own forever (unless my wife sneaks things out of the house) a six-foot-high, spine-leafed Dracaena marginata, probably the ugliest plant in the world. The saleslady called it a "decorator's delight." I've since named it Igor, because I think it might be carnivorous. There are fewer flies in the house since I bought it a year ago, and we haven't seen a turtle I couldn't refuse since the day it got out of its box. To go with the plant, I got an amazing deal on a Great Dane named Caesar (who I know is carnivorous and who sleeps wherever he wants, usually on my bed). In the yard is a genuine 1951 GMC pickup that doesn't run and never will run unless I can find an engine. I bought it anyhow, at a garage sale. "Don't worry, darling," I remember saying. "Think, just think of how much money I was spending on booze. Besides, we can always use it as a planter if I can't find an engine." I also have two lamps (genuine 1934 modern chrome), a folding typing table designed by a maniac (it folds all the time), six new coffeepots (no, I don't know why), a stool made from an old milk can and a tractor seat, a case of canned smoked oysters, and an antique sausage-stuffer with—as nearly as I can figure it—eleven parts missing. There is more—you can buy a lot of stuff in three months or so. But the rest is worth mentioning only as (I wince at the word) junk you trip over.

Thank the Higher Power, the malady doesn't seem to be permanent. I have since quit buying things—unless I need them or at least think I need them. But there is apparently one lasting effect—if not on the drunk, then on the Al-Anon.

The other day, I was in a pet store, and they'd just gotten in some boa constrictors—not too big, perhaps six feet or so. At any rate, I was standing at the glass case looking at them the way you stand and look at snakes, not thinking of buying them or anything, just looking, enjoying the intricate patterns and colors, when I was interrupted by a stifled cry. I turned to see my wife standing in back of me, eyes wide in horror, the twitch definitely pronounced, while her head shook back and forth slowly. "No," she was whispering in terror, "not snakes. Please, not snakes. Anything but snakes."

And that just goes to show, it sometimes takes an Al-Anon longer to get straightened out than it does the alcoholic himself. Hell, I wasn't even thinking of buying a boa constrictor.

Not at the price they were asking.

G.P.
Elbert, Colorado

SECTION TWO

The Miracle of Manageability

" I may have a bad moment, a low hour, or a terrible day, but if I stay dry, the day will pass," says A.H. of Park Forest, Illinois. "I can't afford to get too irritated.... I've gone to sleep with a small resentment and woke up alongside an ugly giant." He then takes us through the rollicking roller coaster of his life as a pianist in a small Dixieland band, an exciting, simple life—and manageable because of our program.

The lives of active alcoholics are typically managed by alcohol, and when the relief of recovery puts the power back in our own hands, it's a sight to behold. One of the story titles in this section suggests, "Let's Take Happiness Out of the Closet." Perceptively observing that "we are not a glum lot" too often takes a back seat to sober-sided sobriety, D.C. of Bend, Oregon, is concerned that some of us feel a member is only working the program if he or she is miserable, and that some of us conjure up a negative thought just to have something to say at a meeting. "I am vowing," she says, "to give loud support to successes, not just encouraging ... troubles and failures. I now see successful living as a natural God-given by-product of successful sobriety. I say, go for it!"

"Thank God, as a result of AA and sobriety, I am liberated from dreaming the impossible dream and free, finally, to start living the possible dream," says J.W. of Islamorada, Florida, who reminds us what it was like to drink in order to transform what seemed like an ugly world.

"All the excitement and interest and wonder of adventure are mine to explore, ever-new, ever-changing, ever-becoming." Ever manageable. This is echoed by a former drama queen from Madison, Wisconsin, who still struggles with what she "might think of as having a 'mundane' life," after living only for the next big event, unaware that all of life is lived moment to moment.

Our quest for manageability never ends. Mary S.'s letter to her husband's morning group is a powerful, poignant reminder that sobriety offers us the ability to manage not only our lives, but our peaceful, sober deaths as well.

Hot Piano Man

May 1953

A s long as I don't take the first drink, the door to this wonderful program remains open. I may have a bad moment, a low hour, or a terrible day, but if I stay dry, the day will pass. Another thing ... I can't afford to get too irritated. I can't choke up. I've gone to sleep with a small resentment and woken up alongside an ugly giant.

So, the prayers, the courage to change the things I can. It's possible for me to get something off my chest if it bothers me. I can talk things out. Sure, I may blow my top at times, even tell someone off. Have to come back to apologize. But don't get so full up to here that a drink is the only out. Don't shut the door.

Well, what's so important about keeping the door open? What's inside? Come on in, take a look for yourself. Meet the wife. Notice she talks freely, and seems at ease. You should see her charleston! It convulses me. But it also gives me joy. Just a bit better than four years ago an AA remarked, "She looks like she's waiting for a knight on a white charger to rescue her." Now get a load of the kids. Every one of them has somethin' goin' on, since the door is open. Saturday morning there may be ten kids in the house, but it ain't too many. I work nights but it don't disturb me. Not joy!

OK. Come on to work with me. Oh, I forgot to tell you. I'm a pianist, and have a small band. We play what is loosely termed "Dixieland" music. I like the room I work in; it's comfortable. Here, sit down anywhere and have some coffee while I do my half–hour set. The band? Yeah, one guy drinks as much and as often as he wants to, and he wants to. Another kind of watches his drinkin'. The third hardly touches the stuff, and fortunately, there's another AA in my band. So live and let live, as long as they play for keeps, and here again the program has knocked me out. What nice guys. Honestly I can't figure it out, not if I figure my efforts alongside of my returns.

Sure I made it the hard way. No hospital; walk the streets; sweat it out; work sober in the same place I'd been drunk in before I stopped; being "not wanted" but sticking it out. Sure I admit it wasn't easy, but good gosh, who'd a thunk I'd get all this on top of escape from the rat-race?

Excuse me, coffee ain't so bad, is it? And they don't overcharge in this joint. Tell me, what is makin' good, being on top? My needs are being met, my bills get paid. Today I'm in good health, I'm playin' my rear end off. That's somethin' I never would be able to do; I'd given up on it. I chose sobriety at the cost of my ability to perform, and listen brother, no one, I mean no one, liked to get knocked out and play music more than I did. And now I'm getting' joy out of sober performance.

Yep, It's a good band, and this is living. It gets quiet inside. I don't talk much about the home within, the me inside, but you get an idea from what you've seen on the outside. "As within, so without."

Now wait a second. Don't start givin' me credit for nothin. All I did was cry like a baby. "Oh God, please help me," and then along came AA, and they told me not to take the first drink, and keep the door open. Yep, the First Step may not be the most important one; not as long as you keep takin' it.

A.H.
Park Forest, Illinois

Let's Take Happiness Out of the Closet

January 1986

The trick in AA is to be happy and then get away with it!" A woman friend with a wry grin said that to me several years ago when I was about three years sober. I did not fully understand her odd sound of isolation or what she was saying. And how could I? I was wallowing in the pain of a lost love, barely making it financially, and confused about my job. She, on the other hand, had it made. She was married, financially secure, owned her own business, and was seven years sober.

Through the next five years of sobriety, my life gradually began to feel better and flow with more ease. At the same time, I noticed an amazing attitude in the general membership of AA toward success. Success made some people nervous, resentful, and distrustful, especially if it was someone else's!

For example, once after a morning meeting, we all met at a restaurant. I was sitting next to an amusing, laughing man. That is, he was laughing until his recovering alcoholic psychotherapist came to our table. Then he didn't feel he had the right to seek professional help and have a moment of gaiety.

Another time I saw a man of about thirty-two come into the AA club wearing a three-piece suit, beaming with purpose. He was a year sober and had finally found the direction and courage to start looking for a job. An old-timer snidely asked if he was going to get too good for us now with his fancy suit, forget where he came from, and end up drunk? Everyone around joined in the laughter (including the young man). However, I noticed the newfound confidence he had brought in with him was gone. He left a few minutes later.

I have watched and heard scenes like this over and over again

in the past few years. It is as if we AAs feel a member is only working the program or doing God's will if he is miserable. I have to ask
myself if AA is that way for me. How many times did I dredge up a
conflict or negative feeling just so I would have something to say at a
meeting? I know I often dwelled on a negative aspect of my life long
enough to have a "good reason" to call a sponsor or a friend. Was I
afraid I wouldn't get the strokes and attention unless I were in some
kind of pain?

After eight years of sobriety, my new husband and I went on our
first sober vacation. (My first ever in forty years of living!) We came
back to our small home group, anxious to share our "funny" stories
about "inept recovering alcoholic vacationers." We soon got the message that our comments about Hawaii met with stony disapproval. It
was intimated we were bragging, even that we shouldn't make others
"less fortunate" feel bad. I began to understand my friend's comment
of years ago, her isolation.

I am living successfully: healthy, happy, and growing. And I think
I should be after all the work I put into learning about myself and
life. If life doesn't start feeling better sober than drunk, why do all the
work and grow through all that pain?

I have to remember that the principle is attraction, rather than
promotion. Thank God there were some sober members living successfully in my early years that I could model my goals after. Thank
God YET stands for You're Eligible, Too.

I have had to fight the compulsion to validate my good life by de-
tailed horror stories about the past, to continually prove, somehow,
that I really am an alcoholic. I have sometimes felt I must apologize
for my happiness.

I am now becoming suspicious of those AA folk who look down
on God's gifts to others. If I can't share my successes with my fellow
AAs, who do I talk to, and how isolated could I end up? I suspect
that some of these people are like I was; never hoping for the good
so when they don't get it, they won't be disappointed or worse yet,
look the fool.

I am vowing, however, to give loud support to successes, not just encouraging pats to troubles and failures. I now see successful living as a natural God-given by-product of successful sobriety. I say, go for it!

Like my friend, I now agree: The real trick in AA is to be happy, and get away with it!

D.C.
Bend, Oregon

The Impossible Dream
November 1971

D uring my days as a practicing alcoholic, I had a maudlin habit that I would guess is uniquely feminine. At some point during the evening, I would weave woozily from the kitchen, fresh drink in hand, and stack a pile of mawkish ballads on the record-player. Then I would settle down to wail my off-key accompaniment. Two or three drinks later, I would be supine, a steady stream of tears coursing across my cheekbones and rolling wetly into my ears as I agonized and empathized with the heartbroken vocalist.

I am grateful for one thing: When the song "The Impossible Dream" came along, I was newly sober. Even sober, I wept over that one! And today, when I play that record, I still feel the old familiar longing for the lovely, perfect things—heroism, chivalry, nobility.

I suspect it is a siren song for many alcoholics, because most of us cherish an impossible dream. Perennially immature as long as we drink, we share with true children an unshakable faith that, if only we find the magic word, we will get the moon for Christmas. Like children, we are prone to tears and tantrums when we don't. Our tears and tantrums require special medication—and all the prescriptions contain a high percentage of alcohol.

In the motion picture *Days of the Wine and Roses,* the alcoholic wife is unable to stop drinking because, she explains, the world is so ugly when you see it sober. I had no trouble identifying with that excuse.

During the years of my sobriety, I have been one of the lucky ones who seldom think of a drink; but, if I like, I can remember what drinking did for me in the early days, the good days. I can remember the release, shyness dissolving, love welling up toward everyone, even myself. I stopped judging and criticizing; the self-defensive chip fell from my shoulder and left me weightless and free; the moon was mine at last, shining silver in my arms and worth whatever it cost!

The only trouble is that inflation sets in early in the impossible dream market. Too soon, for alcoholics, the price skyrockets; the modest hangover escalates to a day home from work, to several days home, to lost job, lost family, accidents, hospitals, jails.

"Why don't you just stop drinking?" our nonalcoholic friends ask when they see our situation. We shrug, and we smile with the charm most alcoholics can muster when necessary, and we change the subject quickly. But, in the dank miasma of the predawn sweats, when we lie sleepless and sick in the rumpled sheets, we ask ourselves the same question, and we cannot reply.

In my opinion, there is an answer—an answer we don't want to face because sobriety also has a high price tag.

We must give up the impossible dream.

For each of us, the impossible dream differs. For one, it may be great wealth; for another, a meteoric rise to fame. For me, it was a world in which love, joy, beauty, and truth (to name a few things) were the rule, not the exception. But for all of us who cherish the impossible dream, it has one common denominator: It is, as the name indicates, a totally unrealistic demand for perfection in one form or another, and it requires of its disciples a fanatical devotion that permits no compromise. We will not settle for less, and we are proud of our refusal.

We look with amused or bitter condescension at the lowly earth people who actually enjoy the mediocrity of their surroundings, their friends, their jobs, their children. Not for us, we say (going to mix another drink); at least we have the perception to spot the manifold flaws in our environment, and the sensitivity to be miserable over them. Never let it be said that we are so lacking in discrimination that we would permit ourselves to enjoy imperfection. So we stagger through the dreary drunken days in pursuit of the impossible dream, worshiping with narcissistic preoccupation our steadfast rejection of the world around us.

Listen to the words of that song the next time you hear it. If they still move you—as they sometimes do me—watch out! Unless you happen to be a nonalcoholic masochist, you are heading for trouble.

After a reasonable number of 24 hours, I have begun to realize certain truths. It is not admirable to rush in where angels fear to tread; it is stupid and self-destructive. It is not heartwarming ideal-ism to hate life for its imperfections; it is rank ingratitude. It is not intellectual superiority to single out the shortcomings of the world; it is self-inflicted, selective blindness. Throughout my drinking years (and for the first arrogant months of my sobriety), I had a field day judging, condemning, and hating. I had to get drunk to escape being poisoned by my own venom.

Eventually, I had to free myself from the impossible dream of a perfect world in order to love and accept the real world. Judged by human standards, life is not perfect; to demand perfection of it is asking the impossible. Life is an incredible totality that ranges from good to evil, from beauty to horror, from bliss to agony. One extreme cannot exist without the other. There would be no music if high C were the only note, no art if red were the only color in the spectrum, no joy in pleasure if pleasure were the only feeling—and, paradoxi-cally, there would be no perfection without imperfection.

What does this mean to me? Well, first it means that I don't have to be perfect. All I have to do is grow at a pace natural to me—and that is all I have a right to expect of others. If I can remember these truths, then love—real love, as opposed to drunken sentimentality—is finally within reach. It is not stupid to accept myself and others complete with our imperfections. It would be stupid not to.

It means that I am free to like and enjoy what I have. I don't need to exhibit my high values by hating my rowboat for not being a yacht, my house for not being a palace, my child for not being a prodigy. In all aspects of my actual life, there is room to grow. More important, my appreciation of what they are now has room to grow. Perfection would limit me; imperfection offers me the freedom of a million potentials. All the excitement and interest and wonder of adventure are mine to explore, ever-new, ever-changing, ever-becoming.

Thank God, as a result of AA and sobriety, I am liberated from dreaming the impossible dream and free, finally, to start living the possible dream.

J.W.
Islamorada, Florida

A Simple Miracle
May 2009 (Excerpt)

Dear Members of the Morning Meeting:

How do I possibly thank a Fellowship that helped my dear husband experience the best three years of his life? Before coming to AA, Paul had experienced a lifetime low, but in recovery he experienced a miraculous rebirth and fully embraced it. With your support he began to regenerate the wonderful people skills he had been blessed with, which I had fallen in love with 38 years ago. When he would come home and circumspectly recount how he had been able to interact with people in need, I would internally smile because I knew the Paul I had fallen in love with in 1966 was resurfacing.

Paul's last three years were his best because he had faced his issues. Freed from his hang-ups and alcohol addiction, he could once again embrace us all. When his illness robbed Paul of his ability to attend meetings, he continued his AA commitment by interacting with

MGH (Mass General Hospital) personnel. Many of them responded to Paul's magic, as sick as he was, by not only talking freely to him as they were treating him, but also returning on their coffee breaks to chat. God bless him, he remained faithful to his AA commitments.

In the end, Paul was granted the grace of a happy death. His entire family—including John in Baghdad over the phone—spent the entire day telling him we loved him and sharing those final precious moments. He was able to love us all and bless us all, and he told me to tell you how much he loved you. Finally, at 7 P.M., he told us he was ready and said, "Buena sera." Those were his final words; he died 45 minutes later.

Please know, Morning Group, that Paul loved every one of you. I know he wishes that you all continue to pursue your recovery and roots for you from a higher place.

Gratefully always,

Mary S.

Life in the Express Lane

(from Dear Grapevine) May 2009

When you are in a 10-items-or-less line in a supermarket checkout, and the person in front of you has more than 10 items and that no longer bothers you, that's acceptance.

If you no longer count the numbers of items the person in front of you is buying, that's serenity.

Paul K.
Merlin, Oregon

Drama Queen
November 2010

I am one of those people who have lived under the assumption that only "big" and unusual events define one's life. One might say that I have a flair for the dramatic. Others have simply called me a "drama queen." And, truth be told, I have had a number of those unusual or profound life-changing experiences, such as growing up adjacent to one of the largest slums in the Philippines, witnessing as friends of my parents were arrested for questioning the justice of a dictatorship, hitchhiking through war-torn Guatemala the summer I graduated from college, getting married after a whirlwind romance, giving birth, getting divorced, being present at the death of my beloved grandmother, descending into the hell of addiction, and miraculously living through it to enter recovery.

These events, and others like them, did indeed help define who I am today, and I love telling stories about my adventures and the "earthmoving" realizations I came to during or immediately following them. However, the importance I have placed on having huge, unique, breathtaking encounters with life has caused me a great deal of pain. After all, life is simply not made up of one dramatic event after another, and my inability to see beyond that led to chronic depression.

In November 2002, my pain had become so great that suicide became a real option. I felt that I was, at most, a worthless shell of a human being and at the very least, rapidly going crazy. On Nov. 8, 2002, I left work to have some drinks with friends. I told my husband that I would be home soon, certainly in time to put my two young children to bed. Happy hour came and went, as did my friends, but I knew the bartender, so I decided to stay just a little longer. At 3 A.M., after closing down the first bar, giving a wary crowd a solo dance performance at the second bar, unsuccessfully flirting with one of the band members who was young enough to be my kid, trying to convince the waitress at a late-night restaurant to break the law and serve me a beer, I found my way home. This was not unusual. Nor were the hangover and the mortification of fuzzy recall the next morning. What was different was that I really "caved in" that day. I clearly remember sitting on the side of my bed, ashamed, tired, and scared, and finally saying out loud, "I think I have a problem, and I don't know what to do." To me, that was a moment of grace. That evening, I went to my first AA meeting. I have been sober ever since.

For the last two weeks, I have been racking my brain to come up with "the" profound, unusual, "wow" experience to write about for a project I am doing in school. Nowhere in the assignment does it say that it has to been a mind-blowing event. But being the drama queen, I automatically think momentous! (drum roll, bright lights, fireworks).

My mind had been spinning obsessively about the assignment, and I was becoming thoroughly frustrated. I live on the west side of town and was driving across town to get home from school last week. As I crossed the street, I noticed a particular pedestrian. She appeared to be in her 60s but she could very well have been younger. In some aspects, she blended in with the street itself, as she was dressed head to toe in worn-out, washed-out, formless grey clothing. At that moment, however, I was able to see her clearly. She was hunched over, pushing a grocery cart of junk: folded up cardboard boxes, some cloth material, plastic bags that were certainly not full of freshly purchased groceries. She was talking to no one in particular. She seemed insane.

Two seconds is not a lot of time. The two seconds it took me to cross that street had an effect on my life because I was present to see it. I don't know what the woman with the cart really is all about. I do know that many alcoholics and addicts end up on the street. That could have been me. It may even be, at some point, the fate of my own beautiful, addicted child. At that moment I was reminded to be humble, to be gracious and to feel compassion, and every recollection of that experience brings me back to that place.

I am now 47 years old. I live in a house that I own in the suburbs of a small college town. I have gone back to school with the hope of some day becoming a nurse. I regularly attend AA meetings. I have a loving and supportive partner who makes me want to be a better person. I have two teenagers who give me a run for my money but who tell me they love me every day. I still struggle with what I might think of as having a "mundane" life. But I know now that life really is anything but inconsequential.

For many, many years I lived solely for a time in the future— the next big event—or off of the tragedies or amazing accomplishments of the past. I was unaware that all of life is lived moment by moment. Being in recovery allows me to be aware and present in those moments, and every moment provides me with an opportunity for growth.

Mary P.
Madison, Wisconsin

Paying the Price for Improvement
January 1997

I am grateful to be in my twenty-first year of continuous sobriety. Looking back, it's truly amazing that I even made the first month. But my sponsor strongly suggested that I build a solid program of action based on service within the Fellowship of Alcoholics Anonymous. The actions I took in those early years helped change my life. The actions I take today enhance my sobriety and allow me to enjoy more of this great world.

Serving the Fellowship and hanging out in meetings was a good start, my sponsor said. But I must also learn to practice these AA principles in all of my other affairs. That included things like taming my temper with my family, being a better responder at work, and treating everyone with respect. Not easy tasks for a newcomer who didn't know anything about dealing appropriately with others. But one day at a time, improvements have been made.

My sponsor told me that AA would put me back into the mainstream of life and give me the opportunity to be a productive citizen. When I was 23, with almost a year of sobriety (though not completely out of the fog) it was suggested to me by my sponsor, his sponsor, and two other AAs that selling bar supplies was a great vocation for a drunk, but perhaps I should go back to college and learn to do something different in sobriety. Things seemed to click, and four years later I'd earned a college education. With this new training, and no plan of action for my life, I set out across the country in search of something.

Instead of really getting into the mainstream, however, I became more involved with general service work. Occasionally I did become involved with civic organizations, professional organizations, and church groups, but these "outside" activities were never really fulfilling, and I always returned to the comfort of activity within the Fellowship of Alcoholics Anonymous.

Doing an inventory with a sponsor on a regular basis is a valuable tool, and it was during one of these six-month inventories when it dawned on me that I'd dragged a lot of garbage with me into my sobriety. I still had a bad attitude after several years of sobriety. Yes, I'd improved tremendously over the person I was when I was drinking, but I still had low self-esteem and a negative outlook on life. I decided to get into action to improve this situation.

As my attitude began to slowly improve, I realized I'd lost my zest for life and that I had no real energy. I looked at my sedentary occupation, my eating habits, and my exercise program, and discovered I was really in bad shape physically. I started working on improving my health and have since discovered new energy along with an improvement in my mental outlook.

My professional life was the next thing that needed attention. Reviewing the different jobs and different states where I'd lived during sobriety made me realize that my resume still looked like that of a practicing alcoholic. Part of the problem was due to the fact that I'd never developed a career plan and hadn't properly prepared to become successful professionally. An AA with long-term sobriety and much service work (he was a past regional trustee) once told me that I should take the time necessary to upgrade my skills and get additional education so that I could be a good provider for my family and find a rewarding career. I remember disagreeing and saying, "AA service work is important to my sobriety." He said that I already had a program solid enough to maintain my sobriety; I'd served the Fellowship, and I could serve the Fellowship again after my professional life and family life were in order. But I still had the attitude that going back to school would cost too much and take too much time. Besides, I thought, what does this old guy know about my situation, anyway?

Today, with my changed mental attitude and improved physical health, I'm willing to pay the price to improve my professional life, and God willing, one day at a time, I'll succeed, and a better quality of life will emerge for my family and me. I now understand what my first sponsor was trying to tell me, and I know now that the old-timer was right. Man, was I slow to get this one!

The program of action that my original sponsor taught to me still works. It works for changing my life, for improving relationships, and for serving others. It works for changing my attitude, my health, and my present career situation. Another old-timer I knew used to say, "Sobriety is a constant process of uncovering, discovering, and discarding." The program doesn't wear out. If there's any area of my life that isn't right, I can apply the principles of the program of Alcoholics Anonymous and begin at once to work toward the desired results. When I'm willing to pay the price for top-shelf sobriety, "action" is still the magic word.

Paul F.
Craig, Colorado

What Used to Baffle Us

I t may not occur to us when we land in AA, escaping from the unbearable, that one of the precious skills we will learn is how to be comfortable with discomfort. But that's exactly what M. McF. tells us. "For the first time, I am learning how to cope with life, people, situations, not as I want them to be, but as they really are." And that results in "a living, challenging, and truly wonderful sobriety."

This theme is echoed throughout this chapter, since it illuminates one of the most promising parts of the Promises. "The world seems lost and wandering again now, but we are the lucky ones," writes G.E.H. of Cumbria in a 1975 story, even if "from the cradle to the grave there is always something wrong somewhere, something to rob us of enjoying perfection, something to bother us." Something to baffle us.

J.F. in Elmhurst, New York, writes that he never knew what to do with "a pain in my feelings," and now "when I start to get emotionally or mentally ill from indigestion of the mind, I prescribe more AA for myself. Better still, I try now to recognize the symptoms and prevent the attack." In the case of Jamie C. from West Henrietta, New York, a visit to the doctor before it becomes an emergency, actually following a sponsor's suggestions, is a brand new, sober way of doing things.

"My apologies, no matter how sincere, were not enough," says a writer about his family. "I had to find new ways of communicating with them." That includes troublesome old Aunt Margaret, who teaches him how to forgive people even if they don't ask for forgiveness. Greg P. of San José picks up a four-year coin and remembers "that I have learned how to be a best friend to myself and that I have four years of learning how and actively trusting that part of me that was once so alien, and that I have stopped feeling ashamed of my disease and have begun to view it as a strength instead of a weakness or failing."

Also in this section we are reminded that screaming safely is one way of handling problems that used to baffle us. "Generally speaking, a good scream works any time the frustration level becomes unreasonable—say, if you stub your toe and land on your trick knee in a mud puddle while you are wearing a good suit."

Enjoy. And keep coming.

Reality Can Be Uncomfortable

July 1971

I s comfortable sobriety the new goal in AA? It would seem so from some of the things I have heard recently, during and after meetings. For instance, at a Step meeting, a young man rather proudly announced that he couldn't possibly take the Fourth and Fifth Steps because "raking up all that stuff would make me uncomfortable." Perhaps it is significant that this same young man was practically always in a state of depression and, after meetings, ran from one member to another asking, "How long does it take to find the joy and happiness in AA?"

A woman AA friend was quite upset because the local AA intergroup office phoned and asked her to make a Twelfth Step call on a very sick girl, who had just made her first appeal for help. The AA member had refused, on the basis that "being around drunks makes me feel very uncomfortable." What a tragic loss, not only for the sick girl, but for the member who walked away from an AA opportunity.

Another member, a man, has been unemployed since a short time before he came to AA, two years ago. He has specialized talent and training and undoubtedly could find a well-paying job and support his family adequately—but he hasn't looked for work because he is "uncomfortable with non-AAs." So he spends all his days at an AA club and his evenings at AA meetings. His favorite plaint to all who will listen is that his family doesn't appreciate him; he can't understand why they aren't impressed with his sobriety. How could they be? He is never at home; he keeps himself wrapped in the comfortable cocoon that is his idea of AA.

There are many examples of AAs who make similar choices in their lives, in favor of the status quo, of remaining "comfortable."

This is not for me! All my life, I have been uncomfortable in social situations, new schools, new jobs—anything unexpected. So what happened? To ease this discomfort, I drank—and finally drank myself right into alcoholism and, fortunately, AA. My sponsor told me that if I stayed away from the first drink a day at a time and followed the suggested Twelve Steps, I could lead a sober life. She didn't promise me health, wealth, happiness, love—or comfort. All she promised me was sobriety! Thank goodness, she didn't promise me anything else, because along the AA path I have found sickness, death, unhappiness, and considerable discomfort. But I have also found the greatest joy, love, and happiness of my life.

For the first time, I am learning how to cope with life, people, and situations, not as I want them to be, but as they really are. Many times, this means accepting a challenge and perhaps being uncomfortable. But it also means accepting life, rather than hiding in AA in order to evade people or situations.

If your goal is "comfortable sobriety"—enjoy it. As for me, I want to continue growing up to new experiences and a living, challenging, and truly wonderful sobriety

M.McF.
Millburn, New Jersey

The Great Art of Living
(from PO Box 1980) June 1975

The world seems lost and wandering again now, but we are the lucky ones; we have the AA program to help us rise above it, and in spite of it.

If we hope that things will one day work out perfectly, we are mistaken. Does that depress you? It needn't, for the fact is, from the cradle to the grave there is always something wrong somewhere, something to rob us of enjoying perfection, something to bother us. When we put one thing right, another will surely go wrong sooner or later. So it behooves us to enjoy every minute we can, for a minute lost is a minute gone forever.

The happiest folk are not the folk without a care in the world; they are the folk who have a genius for happiness, and enjoy themselves even though quite a few things are wrong. The great art of living is to make the best of things as they are.

G.E.H.
Cumbria

Got a Pain in Your Feelings?
March 1950

've been in AA, and sober, for five years. But I still bruise easily—at times. Just when I think God is in heaven and the goose hangs high, something is said or done and—ouch!—I've got a pain in my feelings again!

Ever have that happen to you, a pain in your feelings, just when you had begun to pride yourself on your forbearance and humility? If so, you and I are brothers under our alcoholic skins.

What causes it is immaterial. Whether my grievance is real or imaginary, is of no consequence. Whether I'm right or wrong, I haven't the kind of temperament that can handle a resentment.

It has been my observation that a pain in our feelings can easily become, and often does, the pain of an alcoholic hangover and remorse. Most of us have a low boiling point. It doesn't take much, unless we're careful, to get up a full head of steam in short order. Leave it to us to dramatize or accentuate something out of all proportion to its actuality or significance.

Something derogatory, perhaps, is said about us. We suffer from an unjust accusation. The sincerity of our motives is questioned. Someone doubts our ability to stay sober even in AA. An individual refuses to forgive us or to try to understand our efforts at rehabilitation. We get a bad break at home or on the job. Or a person is unkind or maliciously mean. Our animosity is aroused. We put ourselves on the defensive. A resentment or bitterness is stirred up that can upset our emotional balance.

A pain in our feelings (and that's all it is, really) is preventable if we pause to remember in time just one thing—namely, that a man or a woman, and specifically the alcoholic, is his or her own worst enemy.

If someone were to take the food out of our children's mouths, get us dispossessed from our homes for non-payment of rent, inflict alcoholic convulsions or D.T.s on us, have us thrown into jails or hospitals, or otherwise mistreat us inhumanely, we would look upon him as a monster.

If he were to blacken our reputation, destroy our personal integrity, cheapen our self-respect or make us lie, cheat, two-time, or double-cross, we would be right in looking upon him as monstrously evil and diabolical, with destructive powers.

Has anyone ever done all or many of those things to you or me? No! But we've done them to ourselves while the craving for alcohol was upon us. No one has ever harmed us the way we've harmed ourselves, our families, and our friends.

Let's think of that the next time we begin to get a pain in our feelings about injustices, the criticisms of others, or the realities of life.

Why should I, for example, be resentful against truths, gossip, or malice of others when I was my own worst enemy in the past? When I hurt myself and my family far beyond the power of any friend, relative, or stranger to do likewise?

Personally, I look upon a pain in my feelings as temporary indigestion of the mind. When I get a stomachache, it is generally because I've eaten something that hasn't agreed with me. Likewise, my mental indigestion comes from some story, bit of gossip, or circumstance that I've swallowed without thinking.

When I'm in physical pain, I get relief by medication. When I start to get emotionally or mentally ill from indigestion of the mind, I prescribe more AA for myself. Better still, I try now to recognize the symptoms and prevent the attack.

The next time you feel hurt, outraged, bitter, or resentful—the beginning of many a slip as attested to by AA speakers—try to remember quickly that you haven't been mortally harmed.

In nearly all cases, it's just a pain in your feelings!

J.F.
Elmhurst, New York

Step Ten: Up Close and Personal
October 2007

don't like going to doctors. But this sponsor of mine has a rule: if it bleeds, swells, or hurts for more than twenty-four hours, call a doctor.

So, "Call your doctor," was his suggestion when, one day, I casually mentioned a dull pain around my right ear, an annoyance more than anything, although at times it throbbed a bit. And no, I didn't know why it was hurting, though I thought it might have had something to do with swimming a couple days earlier and, yes, it had been going on for a few days.

I've heard that some people do what their sponsors suggest at breakneck speed, but I'm not in that group. A week went by, and my sponsor said, "How's the pain? Have you called your doctor yet?" I answered the questions in order: "Still as it was, but not getting any worse" and, "No; I tried, but his phone was busy." Silence from him. Then: "Don't you think you need to do a little more work on your Tenth Step?"

Tenth Step? What did the Tenth Step have to do with it? Personal inventory ... when wrong ... admitted it. What did this have to do with an earache? "Just read the Step," he suggested. "You've heard the words at every meeting. But maybe you need to understand more of what they mean." So I did what was suggested. Not at breakneck speed, of course, but I did it.

"Continued to take personal inventory": "Continued" was easy

enough, since it refers to an ongoing process I do frequently—sometimes daily or even minute-by-minute. "Inventory" was also easy. It
was an echo of the Fourth Step, where I did an inventory of myself.

But then I noticed a difference. It was always there, so how did I
miss it? In the Fourth Step, the inventory was "moral"; in the Tenth
Step, it is "personal." Was the different wording significant?

Perhaps it was; perhaps more than I'd first noticed. Bill W. warned
us against complacency or self-congratulation ("After Twenty-Five
Years," Grapevine, March 1960) and reminded us that, unless we keep
growing, we fall back. It seems to me that one of the major purposes
of the last three Steps is to keep us from complacency, to keep us
growing so that we don't fall back into our old, sick ways and perhaps
even into active alcoholism. Of course, that growth needs to continue
on the moral level and we need to "inventory" it. But my inventory,
and growth, also need to include all that I am as a "person," and that
includes my spiritual, mental, emotional, and physical dimensions,
to say nothing of how I relate to other people. And so, taking a "personal" inventory means that I attend to all aspects of myself, of my
"person," including, but not only, the "moral" part of me.

"And when we were wrong, promptly admitted it." Over the years,
how often had I heard that line and misunderstood it? At first, I
thought that it meant to pay attention only to my faults or character
defects. But that's not what the Step says; and, in fact, in the "Twelve
and Twelve," Bill W. writes that we need to be aware not only of our
limitations, defects, and shortcomings, but also of our strengths, tal-
ents, and successes. In short, we need to take a balanced approach
to ourselves. Should my "personal inventory" reveal that I am off-
balance in any aspect of myself, I should "promptly admit it."

"Admit it": This is not a mere acknowledgment that something
about my person is off-balance, that some aspect of me needs correcting, but, once that's done, I must take action on restoring the
balance. From first to last, AA is a program of action. It is not particularly useful for me simply to admit that some aspect of myself
needs correcting and then to do nothing about it. Admission that

something is the matter is the doorway to growth; but there will be no growth unless I follow up the admission with action.

My meditation on the Tenth Step showed me some powerful ways of applying it to my life that I had not seen before. Since alcoholism is an illness that affects all aspects of me, recovery from alcoholism must then include all aspects of me. For me, working the Tenth Step properly means being attentive to my moral growth—as well as my spiritual life, my mental and physical health, my emotional well-being, and my relationships with others. Should I find anything "wrong" about any of these aspects of me, I need to correct it as soon as I can.

"How's the pain now?" my sponsor asked some weeks later. "Gone," I replied. "Ear infection. Good antibiotics. Good doctor." And, I thought, Great Tenth Step!

Jamie C.
West Henrietta, New York

Four Years

December 2010

Monday night I got my chip. It is a four-year chip and it signifies simply that it has been four years since my life changed, four years as a survivor of a suicide attempt that was the end result of an active disease known as alcoholism.

I first viewed alcohol as a friend, a nice aid to help me with the emotional roller-coaster of the end of a relationship. It also served to help me sleep during that time. I had had the mistaken belief, because of an afternoon school special on TV years before, that it took at least four years of heavy drinking to make an alcoholic. To my view, I had only been doing that for about five months, so I still had a good three years to go before I needed to start cutting back.

What eventually happened was that I became despondent and

drank to excess nightly. One day after getting off work, I drank, blacked out, and thought it would be a good time to just end it all with a massive overdose. I came to four days later in the hospital.

At first I was convinced that my problem was simply an inability to keep from harming myself. I was suicidal and I needed help for that. I was suicidal because of my breakup five months before.

However, the only treatment my HMO offered was group therapy every day, in a chemical dependency recovery unit as an outpatient. At that point, with my close brush with death, I figured I needed any kind of therapy that I could get. I didn't really care if it was for people who ate too many snacks and tried to shoot presidents, I needed anything that would not allow me to be alone with myself. I could no longer trust who I was because I had tried to die.

I had always been afraid of death. I was terrified of it and it was inconceivable to me that I would try to bring about my own end. But the group therapy in this type of group, after four days, made me realize that the attempt had happened after a bout of heavy drinking and in a blackout, and that was not normal. On Christmas day 2004 I realized that I was, clinically, an alcoholic.

I was devastated. I had always had my own opinion of what an alcoholic was. It obviously was someone who was weak-willed and immoral. But that could not have been further from the truth.

For an alcoholic, no amount of "will" can keep one from drinking again and again when the disease has reached a certain stage. It is an obsession of the mind and a craving of the body. The only hope is to beat it into remission and that requires very hard and intensive work.

Now I see that my alcoholism was an inability to handle life in an ordinary way, which resulted in an inability to keep from harming myself.

So when I picked up that four-year chip on Monday, it moved me. It reminded me that I had added four years of full living to my life that had come pretty close to extinction. It reminded me that I have learned how to be a best friend to myself and that I have four years of learning how and actively trusting that part of me that was once so alien, and that I have stopped feeling ashamed of my disease and have begun to view it as a strength instead of a weakness or failing.

How? Because for me, it means that I have learned to face some of my own dark monsters and have accepted them to the point that I can move past them. That I have developed a pattern of relating to my world that actually works, without harming myself or others in the process, and that I have learned to do so without the aid of alcohol. I am not my disease; I just have it. I have learned how to live and I have started doing so.

Greg P.
San José, California

Scream!
April 1975

Once the initial step is made (old Step One), and you're over the hump and on the way to recovery, and after the honeymoon—when damn near nothing can bother you—you suddenly find yourself in a strange world, where it's necessary to cope with the problems of life in a completely new way: You have to do it without booze.

Different people, naturally, use different methods. Some old-timers get an incredible, beatific smile and—using a secret method I haven't found yet—turn the whole mess over to their Higher Power, whose shoulders are strong enough for anything. Others make a meeting, or two meetings, or fifty—depending on the size of their problems. Many grab a phone and pick up the power of somebody else who has had to handle a problem without booze. All good methods—but for some members, they just don't quite get it done.

I, for instance, scream. This was not my first choice. Indeed, for the going-on-two years that I've been sober, I've experimented widely, with an intensity surpassed only by the intensity I used to drink with. I had some initial success with curling into a fetal position and sucking my thumb, but it caused my wife embarrassment when I did it at a party. She tried to pretend she didn't know me and, when that didn't seem to work, explained to all the people that I was a writer and that every time I got a new idea for a novel, I acted this way.

So I scream. It was either that or start going places alone, and everybody knows how bad it is for an alcoholic to be alone. I would like to expound on the many benefits of screaming as a means of fast relief from problems. It's handy, doesn't cost much, and takes virtually no time at all to bring into effect—unlike getting to a meeting or trying to phone a fellow AA whose line is busy. If you're thinking of trying it, however, a few helpful hints might ease the way.

First, don't hold it down. Really scream. Otherwise, the desired effect usually isn't achieved. A muffled urk or squeal serves only to make the frustration deeper. Reach down into your guts and pull out a bellow that rips the air, thunders around your head, and makes every hair on people's necks jump to attention. If you're going to scream, scream right.

Now, here is a secondary point on the screaming remedy: when to use it. I've found that the big problems tend to take care of themselves, or that old HP steps in before they get out of hand. No, big problems don't require a scream. It's the little nasties that can grind you down.

A classic example is what I now term The Morning of the Runny Eggs. While I was dressing, the back pocket ripped loose from my new pants when I put my billfold in. I broke a shoelace while tying my shoes. I sat down to breakfast, and my wife had goofed and left the eggs runny. At that moment, I could feel it building. Runny eggs make me ill. But I ate them anyway—the way you do, pushing the runny stuff away with a corner of toast—and had things held almost in control until I walked outside and saw a brand-new tire on the left rear of my car flat. On the bottom. On the same list where runny eggs are number one, tires flat on the bottom come in a damn close two, and it was too much for me to take.

Feeling the frustration building to a danger level, I threw back my head, closed my eyes, opened my mouth, and let out pretty close to a record-breaker of a scream. My throat was sore for two days; my wife said the window above the kitchen sink actually rattled; and—miracle of miracles—my frustration vanished. Unfortunately, my small, sweet border collie, who has big brown eyes and is gentle and was the only one who used to love me when I was drinking, happened to be following me, the way she usually did, when I cut loose. To put it mildly, she wasn't ready. Most of her hair will grow back in time, but I don't think she'll ever again follow me out to the car, or anywhere else.

That incident brings up the final point on using screams for immediate relief of problems. Placement of the scream can be all important. If you get stopped for a traffic violation, for instance (and isn't it wonderful that you can't be nailed for drunk driving?), it is most decidedly not wise to let a scream roar out while the policeman is writing out the ticket. He might break his ballpoint. And everybody knows how those boys hate breaking their ballpoints. Wait until he's given you the ticket and gone down the road, around a bend; then open up and let go. You might scare the hell out of a truck driver or a tourist driving by, but that's a lot better than making a cop break his ballpoint pen.

The only other thing about screaming is knowing when it will or will not feel right. Generally speaking, a good scream works any time the frustration level becomes unreasonable—say, if you stub your toe and land on your trick knee in a mud puddle while you are wearing a good suit.

Or if you're doing a short piece for the Grapevine and it starts to get out of hand and gets longer and longer, when you know they only want short pieces, and you suddenly realize with mounting panic that you have absolutely no way of ending it and that it could just go on and on maybe forever, a whole, epic, thousand-page work on screaming while your family starves and you just keep sitting there writing away about.... Aaaaarrrrggggghhh!

G.P.
Elbert, Colorado

The Fire Has Gone Out
September 1997

I didn't have to be told that in the years of my drinking I damaged those closest to me. My wife's tears and the pain on my children's faces as I erupted again and again in alcoholic rage played a large part in bringing me to crisis and then into recovery. I knew I needed to make amends to them. I wanted to put my involvement with my family on a healthy, functioning, and mutually rewarding basis. There was work to be done, and lots of it.

The Big Book turned out to be right: My wife and children were generous in accepting my apologies, eager to help me heal, happy that the long nightmare in which we all had lived was now over. But that was only the beginning of the process of making amends to them. My apologies, no matter how sincere, were not enough. I'd damaged my loved ones and deprived them of the kind of husband and father they had a right to expect; now I needed to grow out of self-centeredness and selfishness, and to learn to look at the world from their point of view in order to understand what I might do for them. I had to find new ways of communicating with them. All of this took time, to say nothing of that rare quality, patience! It wasn't by accident, I realized, that we undertake the Ninth Step only after we ourselves have become strong enough to embark on the kind of spiritual work that amends-making requires. Perhaps we can expect the Promises to come true only after we've started making amends within the family.

As difficult as this process sometimes was in relation to my wife and children, it took on a new dimension when I turned to making amends within my family of origin. In my own immediate family, the major damages were done by me, and I was the one who needed for-giveness. But there had been no knights in shining armor in my family of origin. My alcoholic father damaged my codependent mother and she damaged him; frightened and angry as I was, I damaged both of them and they damaged me. Aunts and uncles and cousins and grandparents—mutual damages seemed to be everywhere. Everyone was a player, and in all honesty—perhaps because I'd left home in my mid-teens—my contribution to those damages had been relatively small.

But I still needed to clean my side of the street, and I saw that I had to begin by forgiving those who had hurt me. With smoldering resentments still eating at me, I couldn't be really effective in making amends. I hadn't expected it, but forgiving others for the injury they had done to me was a necessary part of my Ninth Step.

But what would it mean for me to forgive those relatives of mine who had made my childhood so unhappy? Clearly it was more than merely mouthing the words, "I forgive you." But what more? And how was it to be done? The Big Book, so helpful in many other matters, didn't really give me the direction I needed. Neither did the "Twelve and Twelve." In a small handful of places, both sources mentioned the necessity of forgiveness—of asking forgiveness of God and of other people, for example, and of forgiving others as well as oneself. In two places, the Big Book even implied that we should forgive and forget. Forget? Forget being beaten? Forget being sexually molested? Forget being neglected? Forget being publicly ridiculed and shamed? These childhood experiences were burned into my memory. Even if I could forgive those who had harmed me in these ways—and the Big Book, unfortunately, didn't tell me how to do that—I didn't think forgetting would be possible.

It turned out, however, that after eleven years in AA, I learned something about forgiving someone, and also what forgiveness means. I learned this lesson by finding myself in a kind of do-or-die situation in which forgiving turned out to be the only good option available.

My mother had died suddenly and I had to return to my original home for her funeral. In the confusion of the next few days, one idea kept nagging at me: I would have to meet, I would have to be involved with, my father's sister, Aunt Margaret. Aunt Margaret! During my childhood, although she was sometimes kind to me (but there weren't many of those times), she was more often unkind, missing no opportunity to criticize me cruelly, even to the point of publicly embarrassing me. Negative in her attitude toward me, bullying, judgmental, insensitive, at times malicious—all of these came with Aunt Margaret. In my mind she'd become a living symbol of much of what my unhappy childhood involved. To have to deal with her—and I could no more avoid doing that than I could avoid going to my mother's funeral—was to raise the ghosts of an unhappy past.

Frankly, I didn't have the emotional or spiritual "energy" to handle Aunt Margaret on top of my own confused and conflicted feelings over my mother's death. "I don't know how I can do this," I said to my sponsor. "I don't know how I can handle the funeral, that whole crazy and sick family of mine, and Aunt Margaret at the same time!"

"Can you try to change the way you see her?" he asked. "Can you see her not as the tormentor of your childhood, but as a pathetic human being who has always wanted something she never got in your grandparents' alcoholic household—simply to be loved for herself? Can you reach around your own pain and touch her hurting spirit? Can you show love to her?"

"But I don't love her," I replied.

"I didn't ask you to love her," he said. "I'm suggesting that you act lovingly toward her, or at least try." I remember thinking: I can try—but it won't work.

I had no sooner arrived at my family's house, where I stayed during the funeral period, when the door opened and there was Aunt Margaret, an odd half-smile on her face. Here it is, I thought. This is it. God, give me some help with this. I went to her. "How kind of you to come," I said. "Thank you for doing this for me. It is very good of you." I hugged her close. (I didn't lie. Everything I said was true.) Aunt Margaret began to cry and I did too. She loved my mother and she was grieving. The old dragon was then just an old lady, perhaps frightened that her own death might not be very far away. Some time later that evening, as she was leaving, I said to her, "I'm going to the funeral home tomorrow to make final arrangements. I'd really appreciate it if you'd come with me to help me through it." She readily agreed (was she surprised I had asked her?), and that established what was to be the pattern of my involvement with her over the next few days. I took opportunities to invite Aunt Margaret to be with me, whatever it was I was doing. I was signaling that I wanted to have her by my side. I was behaving lovingly.

Since then, seven years ago, there have been changes, significant ones, I think, in our relationship. I call Aunt Margaret on Mother's Day and at Christmas and on her birthday. When her husband died suddenly, I called frequently. She writes me and I write back. No, she's still not my favorite person and it hasn't happened that I've come to like her, much less develop a warm, intimate relationship with her. Perhaps it never will. Perhaps, too, it would be different if I were living near to her rather than across thousands of miles, and had to relate to her frequently and face-to-face. That might severely test my resolve to keep acting lovingly toward her! But the reality is that while memories of the past flicker from time to time, the pain of those memories is no longer there. The fire has gone out.

In all of this, Aunt Margaret never once asked for my forgiveness. Probably she doesn't know that she needs any forgiveness from me. So I've learned the surprising truth that I can forgive people even if they don't ask for my forgiveness, even if they don't realize that they need it. Forgiveness seems to depend more on the love of the one who does the forgiving than on the lovableness of the one being forgiven.

One last learning. I discovered that there is a meaning of remembering that goes beyond its minimal sense of just being able to recall. To remember in this sense means to refuse to let go—to keep something from the past alive, to give it weight in the here-and-now. In that sense, I no longer remember the pain Aunt Margaret caused me. I've forgotten it.

Jamie C.
West Henrietta, New York

Gimme Shelter

March 2010

After living rurally for six years with my two daughters, it became necessary for me to move back to Christchurch, New Zealand. I had eight weeks to prepare for moving and I looked at many homes. They far exceeded what I could afford. My past behavior, when looking for property, was to rent what I wanted and get the nicest home, despite the burden it would cause the family financially. This time my thoughts had changed. I could not afford to rent anything that I had viewed so far. Doing so would take the food from our bellies, clothing from our backs, and heat from our bodies during the bitter winter months: My thoughtless actions would cripple the family.

I put the problem in my Higher Power's hands and I put my name down on a government listing for a home. My need wasn't considered urgent and I could be waiting at least a year before a place became available. "Keep us informed," said the housing officer, "of any changes to your circumstances." I kept up my search for a property.

Several incidents occurred. My estranged husband, actively alcoholic and suicidal, went missing; my car's gearbox failed; and my oldest daughter was in a car accident. She had missed payments on her insurance. Also, my elderly mother fell. As I kept notifying the housing officer of the changes in my affairs, I felt his looks of disbelief.

One morning I awoke and crumbled inside. I just couldn't face another day. I called out to God in tears, "I cannot do this anymore. It's too big for me. Please, I give it all to you!" I did my daily readings and my prayer and meditation. I felt a peace and comfort within me that was hard to explain.

I continued doing what was in front of me. The police found my husband safe in his mother's home, after a four-day bender. We rented a car and I sold my car, getting a very good price for it. My daughter's car went in for repair and negotiations began with the insurance company. I still had not found a home, and the day arrived to move. At the last minute, I found affordable accommodations for us: a tent site just around the road from my mother. We were going to stay in my four-person tent and experience a new adventure. The park had all the amenities that we required, plus the bonus of a playground and a swimming pool. Our belongings went into storage. The move into the tent changed our situation on the housing list—we rose into the urgent register because a tent wasn't permanent housing.

We'd been living comfortably in the tent for six days when my mother died. Prior to my recovery from alcoholism, she and I could not be in the same room for more than five minutes without fighting. But with 14 years' sobriety, I could be with her and do for her what I should have done for so many years.

Over the weekend, I did what was needed with my family and returned each night to the tent with my girls. Several people had offered to house us, but I turned them down. The moments since my mother died were the closest I'd had with the girls. I wanted to stay just where we were. We cried, we laughed, and we shared stories about my mother, their grandmother. It was a beautiful time together in the tent.

When I rang the housing officer to tell him that my mother had died, he said he would do all he could for me. Half an hour later, he called: We had a home. It was too small, but I was going to take what was provided. Then he called back: Another home was available, this time with exactly the requirements I had requested from the agency. Without hesitation, I said, "I'll take it."

I know today that because I kept walking the road of recovery with joy and love, accepting and giving thanks, we were provided for.

I am still in this lovely home. I have landscaped the property with a backyard garden and an area of fruit trees and spring bulbs in remembrance of my mother. With this experience, I truly made the decision to turn my will and my life over to the care of God, and then I got out of the way.

Jennifer P.
Christchurch, New Zealand

More Will Be Revealed

Recovery doesn't happen overnight, and neither does addiction, but we do get some gifts quickly. "After about five months," says one member, "the sensations of genuine feelings began to emerge. I honestly didn't know what these waves were that were washing over me, and feared I was going insane. ... Then, one sunshiny day, I learned how to smile. ... Today I can look upon myself and others with understanding, acceptance, forgiveness, and love. ... Recovery is a wonderland."

"I didn't know I suffered from terminal restlessness," writes another. "I knew nothing about true happiness, not even that I didn't know." He then beautifully describes how he goes after the desired state of emotional sobriety: "[I am] trying to locate myself at the center of the universe, searching for just the right intersection of job, relationship, friends, possessions—a magic geometry of people, places, and things that would let me love myself. ... Sober emotional stamina and patience give me a sense of continuity that I never knew existed when I was drinking and new to AA."

"Life to me is a combination of greatness, ecstasy, awfulness, painful awareness, bewildering blindness, and, at times, awesome clarity," says another, noting that it takes a mature sobriety to deal with it.

Emotional immaturity is by no means a new phenomenon. From a 1940 letter: "In our alcoholic days greedy materialism, hate, self-sufficiency, bitter resentments, and egotism, underscored with alcohol, seemingly compromise the sum total of our self." Then we learned to make "proper distinctions" and "We could not help but feel a genuine elation of the human spirit in being unselfishly kind to someone."

That might be a description of the "quiet place in bright sunshine" that Bill W. writes about in "The Next Frontier."

These uncomfortable states of mind are not restricted to newcomers or active drinkers. It might be a surprise to learn how much sober time this writer has: "*As Bill Sees It* showed me just how full of pride—the negative, not the positive kind—I was; also, the selfishness, the self-centeredness, the superiority complex to cover up the inferiority complex—that puffed-up feeling of being the most important person in the whole wide world."

This member has nineteen years, but because she never left the rooms, she knew where to turn to set herself right: "The night when I finished reading the story "Freedom from Bondage" in the Big Book was so beautiful. I identified completely with this woman, and a sense of peace, serenity, and well-being came over me. ... I know now exactly where I lost myself."

Change to Spare
February 2007

When I was still drinking, longtime friends would sometimes ask what I was up to, and I'd answer that I was in transition. I was a musician and a carpenter who couldn't find enough work, so I bounced from job to job. "It's never boring," I assured anyone who asked. "And everything changes, right?"

Vain about my detachment from career, financial security, or any real focus, I touted what I thought was freedom—that is, until I heard a sober alkie speak about it at a meeting. Until then, I didn't know I suffered from terminal restlessness. "Self-will run riot" is never boring. Neither are fear and chaos and skirmishing through life. I knew nothing about true happiness, not even that I didn't know.

When I got sober and started working the AA program, old drinking friends offered condolences and chemical substitutes while I cleaned up my act. "Don't wanna change too radically, do you?" someone asked. My family wanted to know, "What is he into this time, and how long will this fixation last?"

The loss of a small business, a ten-year marriage, and all my property and money kept me bound to a steady paycheck during my first few years of sobriety. I had a sponsor and a weekly home group, but I also traveled, visited, and test-marketed many other meetings. I was also single, so I kept an open door to relationships.

There was always the next new thing to try, a new page to turn, a new chapter to start, or something else just down the road that would be better than what I had. It would be different this time, too, and it would give me that satisfied feeling that I remembered from the few times when booze got my brain chemistry just right. Drinking taught me that getting to the next level required burning some bridges. So, for years I prepared myself to drop everything, walk away, and start over when the next new thing called.

I didn't see myself trying to locate myself at the center of the universe, searching for just the right intersection of job, relationship, friends, possessions—a magic geometry of people, places, and things that would let me love myself. Given sobriety, a patient sponsor, the willingness to work the Twelve Steps, and eventually some professional help, I slowly came to understand.

Now, I've come to believe.

After twenty years of drinking and eighteen years sober—twelve of those investing time, money, and talent in work that I love, but work that has yet to yield a balanced livelihood—I'm on the threshold of yet another major change: a two-year graduate program that will open a path to a well-established career. This new direction is not something the fly-by-night, under-employed, stoned musician would have been willing to think about, much less act on.

Working the AA program has given me the faith that opportunity, understanding, and growth are inherent to mistakes and misfortune. And success is more a state of heart and mind than a sum total of material assets. I've learned that the best things in life aren't things, so today I pray for my Higher Power's will to be done, and for the power to carry that out.

I'm not burning any bridges this time, either. I'm not leaving behind any baggage, unfinished business, or unfulfilled promises. This change has grown slowly from my sober encounters with risk and adversity. My decision comes after years of prayer and meditation and long talks with other sober alcoholics. This time I'm bringing everything I've learned and most of the people, places, and things that I cherish along with me.

I'm not uprooting myself, turning a corner, or shooting off in a different direction. Rather, I am following an outgrowth and extension of the central fact of my life. Sober emotional stamina and patience give me a sense of continuity that I never knew existed when I was drinking and new to AA. I understand now why Bill W., in

Twelve Steps and Twelve Traditions, considered prayer, meditation, and self-searching to be "intensely practical" and "would no more do without [them] than we would refuse air, food, or sunshine."

With this great set of tools to bring to a new career, this change isn't a magic bullet or a departure. It isn't the solution to all my problems, and it isn't going to fix me.

But man, is it ever gonna be fun!

Anonymous

Recovery is a Wonderland
July 2010

O ne Sunday in 1983, a major turning point occurred in my life when I walked into a convenience store. They were selling a certain brand of beer I liked for the first time in Florida, so I bought a couple of six packs to celebrate. Why do I remember that occasion so well? Once I started drinking that day, I was not able to stop. It was as if I had crossed an invisible line that had always been there; my descent into the abyss began. The abyss was the dark void of pain, shame, fear, and loneliness that had always existed within me. Drinking alcohol somehow made everything bearable, it anesthetized my feelings and let me forget my fears.

Soon I was in complete seclusion, isolating in my apartment. By then, drinking had become my entire life. I lived to drink and drank to live. Alcohol became my lover, best friend, and confidant. Nothing else mattered, except having another drink in my hand.

At times I would try to stop. Professional therapy, rehab, antabuse, controlled drinking, sheer willpower, substituting drugs for drinking, hospitalizations—nothing worked. I had become a prisoner of my own making.

On Saturday, July 23, 1988, I started drinking at noon. By six that night I was in a blackout. I woke up on Tuesday morning with a doctor leaning over me in the intensive care unit of a local hospital.

The doctor said I had taken all my pain pills and was very lucky to be alive.

We talked. For the first time, I opened up to another human being. I surrendered. He listened as I described my feelings of guilt, shame, and remorse about my drinking and using. I poured out my life story: losing both my parents as a young girl, being separated from my biological family, getting adopted against my wishes into a different culture, enduring every form of abuse, going through the death of my son, and numerous life-threatening situations including surviving cancer. Now there was this: the incomprehensible demoralization of alcoholism.

Then the doctor gave me the gift of hope. Twelve-step meetings were brought into the hospital once a week and the doctor suggested that I attend. I went to my first meeting, where I picked up a white chip to signify my desire to quit drinking and start a new way of life. The next week I went back and heard complete strangers telling my story. This is where I belong, I thought; I'm in the right place. Two weeks later, I left the hospital. I continued to go to meetings every night, got a sponsor and began to work the Twelve Steps of Alcoholics Anonymous.

In the process of recovery, I gained insight into myself and the diseases of alcoholism, addiction, and relationships. After about five months, the sensations of genuine feelings began to emerge. I honestly didn't know what these waves were that were washing over me and feared I was going insane.

Then one sunshiny day, I learned how to smile. In the program I've learned that I am not responsible for anyone's happiness except my own. Most importantly, I learned that true happiness is an inside job—this was major growth.

July 24, 2010, will be the 22nd anniversary of my new way of life. The story of my recovery is a story of redemption and rebirth. It's the story of two lives in one.

Today I have become the person I always wanted to be. Today I can look upon myself and others with understanding, acceptance, forgiveness, and love. I have discovered the true meaning of the word joy. The Promises have come true. Recovery is a wonderland.

I attribute my continued sobriety to a blessed state of grace contingent on my spiritual condition. The dictionary's definition of the word grace is "unmerited divine intervention and love." During my most difficult moments, I would often contemplate the words from the old Southern spiritual "Amazing Grace" and somehow that inspiring hymnal always gave me the hope I needed. I have spent years looking everywhere, trying everything to fill the void that existed within me. Nothing worked, until the day when I started working the Twelve Steps and began looking within.

Eve Marie
Brooklyn, New York

Stuck in a Funk
December 2010

After 22 years of sobriety, I started slacking on my meetings, from two to three per week to one meeting per week (my home group meeting). The calls to my sponsor became a little less frequent as well. I started feeling disconnected from Alcoholics Anonymous and all the gifts given to me—God, fellowship, Steps and sponsor—all of which equal sobriety for me.

Aside from the position I hold as intergroup rep for my home group, my service was nil. I got to meetings as they were starting and stopped hanging out for the meeting after the meeting. I stuck around, just not for long, and surely not nearly as long as I had while practicing my "regular" program. I now know this led up to the funk I was to feel as a result.

This totally negative space I was in occurred due to changes in my life while living "life on life's terms" instead of seeking God's directions.

I had learned through Alcoholics Anonymous to accept many of life's changes as positive turns in my recovery, and to grow through them rather than look at the negatives. And so I had to take the action.

I was reminded that if I thoroughly work my program with no half-measures, if some negative thinking did occur, it wouldn't go too far, and I would be able to transition back into positive thinking more smoothly. As usual when in that space, I could not pinpoint the reason for it. I told myself there was no need to analyze: "This too shall pass."

I did not want to drink, but I started to notice that I was handling situations differently—not very well, to say the least. As a result of my lack of willingness to continue working the program that had worked for me, my patience was growing very thin, I was worrying about financial insecurity and I was isolating more and more. Situations that used to baffle me were baffling me once again and I was not handling these situations as I once had when working my program and attending regular meetings. I came to realize, coming out of the negativity, that it would never have progressed as far as it did if I had continued to do what I was doing for my sobriety, because it had been working.

Thank God I was still in a semi-sane state and made the decision to reconnect before it got to the point where I allowed my disease to shut out my awareness. So let me tell you about a few of the "God coincidences" since I made the decision to reconnect.

I went to the monthly intergroup meeting, only because of the commitment I had as intergroup rep for my home group. First—thank you, God—had I not made that prior commitment, I could see myself easily going from one meeting a week to none in my less-than-willing state of mind.

At that meeting, they asked for volunteers to distribute 50 gratitude cans to groups that had not yet picked them up. I immediately snickered to myself, while looking up, knowing that my God was behind that request.

With God on my shoulder giving me a loving nudge, and knowing it would help me to reconnect, I volunteered to take eight gratitude cans to meetings in the Coral Springs area, where I reside. Keep in mind that while I was graciously accepting this volunteer work, my head was telling me, Well, it doesn't mean you have to stay for the meetings; you can just deliver the cans and leave before the meeting starts. Well, don't you know that each time I brought a can to a meeting, I stayed for the meeting. Again I was thinking, I don't have to stay for the whole meeting; I can leave early. Once again, not only did I stay for the whole meeting, I stayed for the "meeting after the meeting" as well. (All except for one meeting; I didn't stay for a men's meeting.) As a result, I made seven meetings I would not have gone to, left to my own devices.

During this time, I went to my home group. On my way to the meeting room, there was a woman standing outside, crying while holding on to her 16-year-old son, telling him she wasn't sure she could go in; she was scared. I asked what she was scared of.

She said she wasn't sure she should be there. I told her son I'd take care of her, that she'd be OK, and he left on his bicycle after telling her he'd be back. I told her it was a friendly group on the other side of the door, and that it was a beginners' meeting. She said, "That's me." I said, "Sounds like a God coincidence to me."

I told her I'd show her where the coffee and pastries were, and I got a couple of seats for us. Then I got a meeting schedule and passed it around to the women for their names and phone numbers for her.

The format of my home group is speaker/discussion. After the speaker, the chairman asked if anyone with zero to three months would like to share. I encouraged her to raise her hand, tell everyone her name and let them know it was her first meeting. She stood up and did just that, and when she sat back down we held each other while she cried.

Just before it was time for chips, I was explaining the chip system to her. She immediately started responding with reasons not to take a chip. "I think I'll wait, go home tonight, think about it, make sure this is something I can do ...." People turned to her, encouraging her.

She made that long walk to pick up the white chip. When she returned to her seat, we once again held each other while she cried.

She was feeling happy that she picked up that white chip! She kept saying thank you as she held the chip up while looking to the sky.

She stayed for the "meeting after the meeting," and her son sat with us. At that time, she shared that she had been to a meeting once before with her son and had a bad experience—someone told her that she hadn't hit her low point yet. Because of that she had no desire to return and hadn't gone to any more AA meetings ... till my home group meeting. She told her son she loved the meeting and everyone there. I let her know that there are over 800 meetings in Broward County, so if she ever has another experience like that, she has many other options for meetings. I also let her son know about Alateen.

As I was saying goodnight to her, she held up her white chip and said, "Laura, this is all because of you." I cut her off and responded with, "This is all because your God chose me as an instrument for you."

Six days have passed. I'm not sure if she attended another meeting since then; I have not heard from her again. She had my phone number.

Needless to say, I am hoping to see her at my home group meeting again. And if I do, I will be getting her phone number for Twelfth Step work to stay connected. Funny thing is, she was so appreciative of me for helping her, but I am even more appreciative of the gift I had that night in helping her—she helped me so much more!

Talk about God working in my life yet again at a time when I'm reconnecting, huh? This is an awesome reminder to me that my God is awesome; that it isn't all about me, it's about helping the newcomer; and that I am so very blessed to be in a position to be able to help others.

Laura S.
Coral Springs, Florida

Carrying the Message— Life!

June 1966

I had difficulty agreeing with the article, "Mental Depression," in the March Grapevine. Doesn't mean that I am right. Just means that my experience and understanding are of a different texture. To me life is far too complex to feel that there is a single answer even with the use of the AA philosophy, as much as I love it all.

Life to me is a combination of greatness, ecstasy, awfulness, painful awareness, bewildering blindness, and, at times, awesome clarity. The whole thing is too gloriously wonderful and awful to seek simple and lasting answers. Temporary answers, yes, but not lasting ones. The temporary answers that come through working the AA program are, to me, breathers until the next dark and glorious episode. Though I struggle, and at times hate it, I would have it no other way.

E.M.M.
San Francisco, California

Mail Call for AAs at Home and Abroad

March 1949

In our alcoholic days greedy materialism, hate, self-sufficiency, bitter resentments, and egotism, underscored with alcohol, seemingly compromised the sum total of our self. We had only a vague notion of the Higher Power.

After we had a spiritual experience through the medium of AA we were brought into closer contact with the Power greater than ourselves. After we had a clear notion of his true significance, he dissipated all our false ideas concerning ourselves and our relation to the universe. He immediately became our tutor and our guardian and revealed great truths to us which changed our materialistic and alcoholic thinking.

We were taught a new philosophy of life. We learned to make proper distinctions and grasp the true meaning of spiritual, moral, and social values, all of which were obscure and meaningless before. For the first time in many years we enjoyed a good book and knew what we were reading about. We recognized the sorry plight of another alcoholic or perhaps a non-alcoholic and rushed to his aid.

We could not help but feel a genuine elation of the human spirit in being unselfishly kind to someone. We found that true morality has its inevitable compensations, for when we benefit someone we increase our own happiness.

God Didn't Follow Orders

July 1984

Two years ago, all hell seemed to break loose in my personal life. At that time, I was approaching my nineteenth year of sobriety, and my life was definitely unmanageable—eighteen years or no eighteen years.

My sponsor and the old-timers had warned me about complacency a long time before. I had to make a commitment to myself.

In the following seven months, I read *As Bill Sees It,* the "Twelve and Twelve," and the Big Book. I honestly couldn't remember the last time I had read any one of those books.

As Bill Sees It showed me just how full of pride—the negative, not the positive kind—I was; also, the selfishness, the self-centeredness, the superiority complex to cover up the inferiority complex—that puffed-up feeling of being the most important person in the whole wide world.

An old-timer in the group I used to belong to would call me Queenie, and he wasn't kidding, either. It used to annoy me no end and even make me mad sometimes! He was merely saying, "Queenie, you're only another little fish in a big pond." But by then, the barriers were so thick and so high he couldn't get through.

As Bill Sees It merely touched the tip of the iceberg. Now it was time to get into the "Twelve and Twelve."

I read the chapters on two Steps each night before going to bed. It was all brand-spankin'-new to me. In my early days of sobriety, I had read the "Twelve and Twelve," but it had an entirely different meaning to me then. This time, different questions were being asked, and different answers were being sought.

Each night after reading, it seemed to me as if part of a veil or curtain was being lifted just a little. The night after reading Steps Seven and Eight, I cried. Step Eight especially had supplied most of the answers. What a tremendous relief! This Step talks about a person's being either on top of the heap or on the bottom of the heap. That was me, all right. The last page of the chapter talks about ending our "isolation from our fellows and from God." That's when I cried.

No specific time nor even a specific year of sobriety can be given when my terrible, terrible feeling of isolation from my fellow human beings and from God began. But it did. The phone hardly ever rang anymore; no one wanted to pick me up for meetings anymore—I had to call a cab to go to one meeting a week. The list could go on and on.

And boy, was I ever mad at God! I was telling him in no uncertain terms exactly what he should do in my life, and he wasn't doing it. The job that was being prayed for so hard didn't come. The aunt who was so seriously ill with a lung disease wasn't healed; she died.

I couldn't go on like that indefinitely.

The night I finished reading Step Twelve, it seemed as if the veils or curtains were all lifted at the same time. I realized I had become exactly what my sponsor and the old-timers had warned me against— a complacent old-timer.

Now, it was time for my next commitment: to read the Big Book. I read two chapters each night, and the Big Book was all brand-spankin'-new to me.

Every night, there would come at least one insight, sometimes more. When I read the prayer regarding total and complete surrender of my life and will, the relief was just that—total and complete. My morning prayers and meditation took on a whole new dimension.

One morning when I was saying my prayers, I thought: Am I ever lucky that God didn't get mad at me when I was praying specifically and giving him orders about my life! He knows, really knows, that I am a human being, and he truly loves me—good and bad. In addition to saying the prayer of surrender in the Third Step every morning, I sincerely admitted that there wasn't one single, solitary character defect or shortcoming that I wanted to hang on to anymore. I started saying the recommended prayer to have my character defects removed. The beautiful results of praying and seeking God's will in my life are far from passive.

Neat things, really neat, started to happen.

My isolation from my God just evaporated.

The telephone started to ring again; I was amazed when I got three calls in one afternoon. One was from a lady I sponsored four years ago. She is still sober, and we had the nicest visit. Before she hung up, she said, "I love you," and I said, "I love you, too." A friend of mine always says, in Bill's words, "AA is 'the language of the heart.'"

Then there were the visits from long-absent friends. After meetings is always the nicest time, when everyone is relaxed, honest, and open. One friend came by one afternoon unexpectedly. When I opened the door, she said, "You look terrible without your makeup!" I wear makeup at meetings, but not at home.

Through a series of phone calls, I was put in touch with acquaintances who were just waiting to become friends. They started to pick me up for meetings—places I've never been to before—several times a week. Each week, it varies.

My isolation from my fellow human beings has also evaporated.

The night when I finished reading the story "Freedom from Bondage" in the Big Book was so beautiful. I identified completely with this woman, and a sense of peace, serenity, and well-being came over me. It was as if I had been pressing a different key each night on a computer, and all of a sudden all of the insights came on the screen. I know now exactly where I lost myself. I know now exactly where my written inventory will begin.

In fact, when I'm all finished writing it, I would like to imagine the old-timer who used to call me Queenie sitting on a white, fluffy cloud in AA heaven with a twinkle in his blue eyes, showing his wry sense of humor, and saying something like: "Well, finally! Nobody has to call her that any longer."

V.P.
Toledo, Ohio

Powerful Simplicity
March 1984

A n old-timer challenged me once: "Can you tell me what love is, in one word?" I thought and thought, and finally gave up. "Energy," he said. I'd been watching this man closely for a long time. The nearer he gets to the down-and-outer in the meeting room, the more he sparks up. He's our group's "unofficial janitor"—always there, serving in a thousand ways. He sponsors new ones and old ones, spent years in H&I (hospital and institution service), and is now active in public information. The other day, he spoke to a sizable group of staff psychiatrists at a local hospital; they stayed over to keep listening to him, gladly missing their lunch hour. They must have been wondering: How can such complexities in human beings be turned into such powerful simplicity?

By love. This old-timer has come to know what it means to be a trusted servant. He's around. There's something in him. A group in our city recently placed these words in our newsletter: "Help! We need old-timers at our meetings." He responded. But he is only one. It was a good reminder for me that all of us, old and new, need one another in gut-level, often desperate, intense ways. Of AA's co-founders,

Bill W. and Dr. Bob, the Big Book says: "Both saw that they must keep spiritually active." And the sentence that follows describes spiritual action: "One day they called up the head nurse of a local hospital. They explained their need ...."

Together. Where can living energy go if it can't find its home between the older and the newer AAs? Sometimes, I've seen that old-timer enter a meeting depressed, for the weight of humanness is no less his than ours. And during the meeting I've watched discomfort lift from his face, to be replaced by a gentle, knowing grin.

Somehow, the inner energy that is love connects all the parts of us—our emotional, mental, physical, and spiritual selves. The first law of physics finds that energy cannot be created or destroyed. It's already all here; it can only be transformed into other energy—"new" energy, always moving, always mysteriously, on its own paths. This energy, or love, permeates the air and our inner lives when we're together; the more we drink it in, the deeper our insights become and the more "moments of perception" we're likely to have, wherein the "roots of reality ... will hold fast despite the high winds of the forces which would destroy us, or which we would use to destroy ourselves." (*As Bill Sees It*).

Another natural law reveals that the whole is equal to more than the sum of its parts. In an appendix of *AA Comes of Age,* when "A Friend Looks at Alcoholics Anonymous," the following line stands out: "For in AA the whole is truly greater than the sum of all its parts. The infusing power of the group, of our Fellowship, draws something more out of each of us than any of us by himself can supply." That certain "something more" must be understood by each of us in our own way, yet it also needs to be passed between us.

I am eternally grateful to old-timers who hang around and challenge me with impossible questions that lead ultimately to the possible quest.

Anonymous
California

SECTION FIVE
___

Rooms of Our Own

B
ack in the 1940s, articles in the Grapevine expressed alarm at the possibility of "old-timers" getting stagnant, even though AA itself was barely in its adolescence. One member, sober for 14 years, writes, "But here I was, sober, healthy, loved, solvent (if barely), but temporarily defeated by monotony, insignificance, and discontent. God had not signed on to my tacit bargain that I'd be a better servant in exchange for a bigger bank account."

Our disease, cunning, baffling, powerful, sneaks up on us, plays three-card monte with us, springs at us from nowhere. "Meetings in the Bank" is a terrifying tale of a member about to undergo surgery and the danger he faced. No, this time it wasn't pain pills putting him in danger. It was a nameless despair, a desperate pessimism, and it took his impressive bankroll of past meetings to prevent him from succumbing to it. It wasn't clear what the voice of despair wanted him to do. But he didn't listen, went ahead with the surgery, and writes:

"After almost four years of limping through life, I walk the Road of Happy Destiny free, light, and out of pain. The walk of a sober man, who recovered from surgery quickly in the middle of the long, slow recovery others have always wished upon him." He wasn't at a meeting, it was too late at night to call anyone, but his long, slow recovery, based solidly in past meetings, came to his rescue.

Consider the Old-Timers

June 1949, By the Editor

Consider AA old-timers—those fellows who've been continuously dry and happy for four, five, six, or more years. Everybody takes them for granted. They have no problems! Or have they? The Number One problem, drinking, has receded almost to the vanishing point. Economically they're pretty well straightened out. Some, in fact, are already working on their second millions. The family snarl, if any, has usually been desnarled either in a reunited brood, a new marriage, or a comfortable retreat to single blessedness.

So what's the problem?

It's not easy to describe. But it's nonetheless a real problem. Some say it's a restlessness, an unsatisfied feeling, an unwilling boredom. It's not mutiny nor is it any criticism of AA. It has come out of nowhere to attack men and women whose faith and good works in AA are beyond all doubt.

All of us have had spells like that but have usually snapped out of them as we came out of a more or less routine depression. Even those oddities of nature, nonalcoholics, have such lows. But a great many AAs have had "it" move right in, perched like a ghoul of gloom on their shoulders, poking its nose into all their affairs. "Hmmmmm! Not having any fun, not getting much lift, eh chum?"

There's little danger of them taking a drink. They're not hysterical. But they are concerned. They blame themselves and keep their vague fears and doubts to themselves. Then, little by little, they begin to find out that others feel the same way—usually along about the fourth or fifth year. Some get it earlier, some later. Some, apparently, never get it.

Frank discussion, getting it out in the open just as they did with their original alcoholic problem, has helped many to understand what has happened. In the early days and years when things are happening with almost breathless rapidity we get a terrific sense of growing. We can feel our personalities change. Progress, real and tangible, can be measured almost by the day. After a while that slows down a bit and we start to take charge of ourselves emotionally. We realize we are becoming adults, at long last.

By this time we've usually done a good share of Twelfth Step work, we've spoken at more meetings than we can count, we've served as group secretaries, on committees, and generally run the gamut of AA activities. Then, consciously or unconsciously, we retire, stand down to let the newcomers take over—an AA Tradition. Then it is, apparently, that we enter into a period of stagnation. We all understand that we don't dare stand still. If we're not growing, we slip back. And any alcoholic should fear that—and fight it.

So what to do? The old old-timers, those WBBB boys (With Bill Before the Book), probably had the same troubles. But they worked them out individually and not much was said or heard about it.

Today, however, AA has reached a point in years and in numbers where there are (estimated) between 10,000 and 15,000 of us who've been dry successfully for four years or longer. What percentage are feeling disquieted and looking for new worlds to conquer there is, of course, no way of knowing. But from a sizable sample it would seem there are enough to make it something to consider on a movement-wide basis.

These people want to do something about it, get together in meetings and apply the old group therapy again, only this time not to the direct problems of alcohol. They don't want to sing any psalms or beat any breasts or preach any sermons. But many feel an urge to dig a little deeper into spiritual matters. So they're going ahead, realizing that they are departing from the AA script somewhat.

No one remembers better than these self same AAs why we don't go too deeply into the spiritual phase of the AA program in our own regular meetings. Because they know that the newcomer, frightened, God-shy and skittish, can easily be scared off. We're all pretty much convinced that, whatever our understanding of God, he smiles his approval on our method of letting each new drunk find his own way.

Yet these old-timers have a new thirst and want to get on with it. Some have done it in small groups, quietly. Others have sought and found help outside AA in their churches. Now another and larger group on Long Island have begun regular meetings, patterned somewhat after the regular AA meetings, but stressing the spiritual.

Some AAs are going to point out that AA is not a cult! They're going to say, and maybe they're right, that if you're looking for God you'll never see him more completely at work than at any AA meeting.

That, in fact, may be what these experimental meetings will prove. If so, fine! These restless old-timers are not attempting to set up an "Advanced AA" with themselves as preceptors. These meetings are open to all, whether dry ten years or ten minutes. These experimenters are willing to face the prospect of utter failure, which itself may teach. After all, AA itself was founded on trial and error.

The AA Grapevine ventures no opinion. We're merely reporting. Whatever comes of this particular project, success or failure, is of minor consequence. The main thing is, that if there's a problem, whether it be a mere growing pain or a genuine ache, that problem is now out in the open.

Easy Does It—Live and Let Live—and by the grace of God, it too will get solved.

Continuance

October 1998

I don't have time for this right now, I thought. But I pushed myself away from my desk and said, "I can't offer any advice that you haven't heard before, James. When it comes to living sober, I've learned that being original doesn't work." These were words that my sponsor had once shared with me.

I was too backed up with work to take time out for this. As I'd told my wife, I was too busy losing money to be there for others. But I also wanted James, my sponsee, to feel better about the problems that filled him with guilt and despair. I felt desperate myself, listening to how much he wanted relief, and knowing I was powerless to change things for him.

Besides, I was wrestling with a few old character defects of my own. Creative work that I'd devoted months to had received unanimous rejection. Washing over me were waves of what, as an active drunk, I used to call depression; I know it better now as hurt pride, envy, resentment, and self-pity.

"It's simple, James," I said. "Stop expecting everything to turn out the way that you demand. In the long term, Steps Four through Nine provide the best plan I've found for taking care of the kind of problem that's bothering you. And to be honest, that's all I understand about how things work. If you want to feel better right away, ask God to help you to be of service. Get to a meeting. Reach out to a newcomer. That's what works for me."

"Yeah, I know," James said impatiently. "I'm going. Tonight, probably."

"Probably, James?" I said. "There's no 'probably' about the disease you and I have. Untreated, it definitely, not probably, destroys us. But my sponsor promised me that I would know a new freedom. My feelings of uselessness and self-pity would disappear. He didn't say 'probably.' He promised. But there are conditions. I have to thoroughly follow the path others have followed." James knew I wasn't doing well financially. I'd been told ten years before that probably I'd have some success in my field. Probably.

These are not the expectations that had propelled my recovery fourteen years before. Self-acceptance, life on life's terms, powerlessness, being right-sized, God's will for me: At the beginning, these were code words for me hitting my stride at last, rising—albeit slowly and with hard work—on my golden dreams of money, power, and prestige. After all, only someone with as much genuine humility as me could properly rededicate such rewards to bringing God's will into being.

But here I was, sober, healthy, loved, solvent (if barely), but temporarily defeated by monotony, insignificance, and discontent. God had not signed on to my tacit bargain that I'd be a better servant in exchange for a bigger bank account. And I was powerless to uplift a new sponsee whose problems seemed to me a simple matter of taking inventory and making amends.

"Hey, I've got an idea," I said. "How about you and I go to a meeting right now? The nooner starts in forty-five minutes. You can go tonight, too."

James had three quick excuses to beg off, none of them convincing.

"There's always something, isn't there, James?" I said.

"What?" he sounded defensive. "You think I'm making this stuff up?"

"No," I said. "I think your disease is. Mine still does. I've just learned to listen to other people's guidance a little better. That's the only difference between you and me—I've had more practice listening to other people's advice. So I've got a frame of reference bigger than the noise in my head."

James rang off with a firmer pledge to make the evening meeting. But he still sounded angry with me.

Which, when I had a moment to think, deepened my own funk. Look at you, sober fourteen years, and you can't sell your work, can't pay your bills, don't have any prudent reserve, and you can't even help another drunk very well either.

That noon meeting was suddenly looking pretty good—even if I was too busy losing money. I hopped in my truck and headed into town. The speaker opened his story with words his sponsor had given him that day: "The best way for me to succeed and grow in sobriety is to follow the advice I hear myself giving others. This is how sponsoring others helps me most."

During the break a friend who works in the same field as I do listened to my complaints about lack of success. He said that he approached doing the work the same way he did sobriety. Regardless of circumstances, you just keep doing it, one day at a time. "Continuance," he called it. "And it helps too to drop out of the debating society. Nobody promised we'd get to understand more about how the universe works than anybody else. Just a little more than we did as miserable drunks."

Yes, I used to be miserable—and lying, thieving, cynical, violent, suicidal. That certainly cast light on my present problems.

Returning to work that afternoon, I already knew I'd be going to the meeting that night as well. Whether or not James made it wasn't important. I needed to. Following my own advice worked better than thinking my way out of my problems. I planned to stick with it for that day. I had the time now.

Anonymous
York Harbor, Maine

Not on Fire
March 2010

Afew days after I came into AA I was at a meeting and the topic was gratitude. With just a couple of days sobriety I was still full of anger, resentment, shame, guilt, and fear. The world had failed to give me what I felt it owed me and everyone in it had let me down. Life was painful and hopeless. I absolutely did not feel grateful for anything!

When it came my turn to share I said, "My name is Regan, and I have nothing to be grateful for, so I'll just pass." The long-timer next to me leaned over and whispered in my ear, "Be grateful you're not on fire." What the heck did that mean?! I turned and glared at him with the meanest look I could muster, but he just smiled at me. That old man and his comment made me even more angry. I still continued going to meetings, listening, and trying to figure out what people were talking about. It took a few weeks, but eventually I began to understand what that man had been trying to tell me.

I had been focused on all the "bad" things in my life. I was pretty much homeless and had been sleeping in cockroach-infested abandoned buildings and even a dumpster before coming back to AA.

I was unemployable, I had no money, and I had lots of legal and financial problems, some of which I was looking at jail time for. I had abandoned my son, destroyed my marriage, and my father had told me that if I ever came near the family again they would call the police. There was nobody who understood how I felt or who even wanted to be around me, let alone help me! Now here I was, living in some halfway house in a town I didn't even like, and sitting in this stupid AA meeting with all these losers! How could anyone be grateful for any of that?

But gradually, I began to see that good things had started happening in my life. True, I still had strained relationships and the same legal and financial problems. But I was sober!

I had a roof over my head and a warm bed to sleep in. I had food to eat and clothes to wear. I was surrounded by people who really understood me and were willing to help me, expecting nothing in return. This is what that old man was saying to me. No matter what is going on in my life, no matter how bad things seem, I can always find something to be grateful for if I just look hard enough.

Even now, many years later, I can still occasionally put myself in a place that seems utterly hopeless with seemingly unbearable circumstances that I am certain I cannot possibly survive.

Then I remember what that old man said and I know there has to be something to be grateful for if I am only willing to change my attitude and look for it.

I might have to start with just being grateful I am not on fire, but once I get that, I can always build from there.

Regan G.
Mesa, Arizona

AA for Two

December 1960

On August 23, 1959, I found myself in a real jam. Not that I hadn't been in a jam most of my life, but this was different. The night before my wife and I had erupted into conflict. It was basic; it was family; it was financial. Thinking it over this next morning I felt inwardly sickened. Here I was, with five years of sobriety, hopeless and powerless. I loved my wife dearly. This breach was frightening and intolerable.

I picked up the Big Book. My eye fell on a passage I had previously marked. It had to do with the taking of Step Three—surrender. It said, "We found it very desirable to take this spiritual Step with an understanding person, such as our wife, best friend, or spiritual adviser."

I deliberated. We were spending the summer in a remote New England countryside. I had no best friend. Then it struck me suddenly that there was a minister, not of my faith, in a nearby village. I had met him once or twice. In fact it was in his church that I had attended AA meetings. Why not approach him? He would be my spiritual adviser. This was a big thought. I was excited. I was about to take a big step.

I got up from my chair and started out the door. I was actually in motion when another thought stopped me. "We found it very desirable to take this spiritual Step with an understanding person, such as our wife ..."

Our wife. My wife is not an alcoholic. We had been married only a few months when I came into AA. She had stuck by me during the horrible, wretched, insane days of my drinking; she had stuck to me faithfully and wondrously all during my AA life. She herself, being sensitive and highly intelligent, had staunchly embraced the AA way of life. Yet when I had read the passage in the book I had flipped her out of my mind. I was angry with her, of course. She had upset me. I would get even with her by by-passing her for a minister whom I barely knew. I didn't reason it out that way. I was too resentful for reasoning.

But now it flashed into my consciousness, that phrase "such as our wife." It jolted me to a standstill. I turned around, marched back into the house and went to my wife. I told her what had happened. I showed her the book. We went over the passage and sat down and discussed ourselves. And then we said a prayer, asking our Higher Power for help. We felt better. We decided then and there that, come hell or high water, we would meet every day and ask our Higher Power for help. We would meet under the scriptural aegis, "whenever two or more of you are gathered in my name ...."

At first our thought was to change the attitude of others toward us. How do you do that? By praying for them. So we prayed for them. Then we began widening the circle of people for whom we prayed. We prayed for everybody. We knew that by making our prayer all inclusive we included ourselves. In a roundabout way we were thus getting closer to the spirit of the Eleventh Step, seeking a conscious contact with our Higher Power.

Tensions, which had been running high in the household, eased off. The odd thing was that our prayers seemed to be affecting others as well as ourselves. There was a decided atmospheric improvement, but months went by without noticeable changes. Then things began to happen—disagreeable things, however, flattening things—one frustration after another—rebuffs so violent and arbitrary that they could not be taken as accidental. A project on which I was working collapsed on the verge of triumphant success; an article on which I had labored was accepted by the editor and turned down by the publisher—our financial condition was worsening. Along in January we made a desperate decision: We would go to the Bahamas and find an inexpensive place to live for the rest of our lives. We had an income, so why not? The only trouble was that the Bahamas proved as costly if not more so than the big city. Searching ourselves ruthlessly we had to conclude we were not very honest, not very sane. We had chosen an expensive resort area in which to economize; we mistook sunshine and beautiful beaches as a cure for spiritual ulcers. As far as worry was concerned we were worse off than before.

We met a missionary priest on one of these islands. I recounted to him our series of rebuffs and said, wryly, that it looked to me as if someone from Mars were trying to signal us.

"Do you really believe that?" said the priest, knowing that my observation was veiled and that by the visitor from Mars I really meant God. I said, "Yes, I do," and he said, "Then you will get your answer. You will be surprised."

This remark kept us in balance through many a dark day. It helped to reinforce our initial decision to make our session a daily practice. Out of the 365 days we missed only one. That was due to a virus at Christmas time. We set aside a period after breakfast, while the day was still fresh with promise. Sometimes this was difficult.

We traveled a lot. At one point we were cruising on a forty–foot yawl in Bahamian waters. The skipper and his wife were the other passengers. The only privacy we had was in our bunks, up forward. We had to snatch a few minutes after waking, leaning across from bunk to bunk, and whispering the "Alcoholics Anonymous is a fellowship of men and women … etc." and a prayer, since anything louder than a whisper could be heard in the calm of our morning anchorage.

At another time, while traveling by bus through the South, we left our hotel one morning in such a rush to catch the bus that we didn't have time for a session and saw no opportunity of having one until nightfall. So at the depot we stood in a huddle before a baggage locker, the door of which was open, and while pretending to be preoccupied with our luggage we managed to engage in a whispered meeting. Well, the missionary was right. It was quite a surprise to find ourselves, four months later, on another island, 5,000 miles away; an island whose name we didn't even know at that time. How we got there is another story, though my wife and I are firmly convinced that those daily sessions are responsible. We had to be uprooted, upturned. I am convinced, too, that only those successions of reversals could have blasted us out of our old habits, our fearsome clinging to what we possessed, even though we knew these possessions were slipping from us.

It happened so simply that we hardly realized it at the time. One day in the Caribbean I was looking through the AA World Directory when I chanced on the name of a loner on an island in the Pacific. He answered fully and completely, and to such satisfaction that we packed up and joined him. And here we found a new life. Economically and in every other way it is beyond our fondest imaginings. Better still, we arrived on the scene as our loner friend was miraculously recovering from near-death-by-accident. We feel we have been helpful to him, and that the opportunity was God-given to us. We are learning to deal with money matters; we are learning, as it is noted in the *Twelve Steps and Twelve Traditions,* to make money our servant rather than our master. We do not expect to be here forever, any more than we expect to be any place forever.

But we are not trying to tell God how to manage us; we are trusting him to tell us. We feel pretty sure that if he could get us onto a Pacific isle he can get us off it if need be.

Anonymous

Meetings in the Bank
June 2009

I n July 2008, I went into the hospital for hip replacement surgery. At the time, I had been sober over 12 years, so I knew to do all the things I was supposed to do, such as share my addiction history with my surgeon and my fears and anxieties with my home group. I talked at length with other people who had gone through similar procedures.

But as someone I admire once said, "We always worry about the wrong things." My worries about pain medication never materialized. Twenty-four hours after surgery, I was off epidural pain meds and onto oral medication. I weaned off the pills steadily and diligently.

You know the old expression about "having meetings in the bank"? I now know what that means. It means having meetings in the bank just in case things turn up to disturb your regular routine, and you can't get to your normal group for a couple of days. It does not apply to the upheaval of surgery. When you're in the hospital for five days, that bank is not accessible. You need visitors, you need the phone.

And here's why. My disease was clever enough to wait for all the program people and doctors and nurse to leave, to make sure I was alone, and to sit on the edge of my hospital bed in the middle of the night—when I had nowhere to go—and tell me the surgery was a mistake and I would never leave alive.

I prayed and breathed and cried and shook my hands to try and brush it away. The only thing that could chase my disease was the sun rising on a new morning. Just like when I was counting days 12-plus years ago, and I would wake up and think, Hey, I made it. Grateful, of course, but willful. As I look back now and then, I wish one of those 2 A.M.s I had picked up the phone and called another alcoholic or intergroup. Maybe you will.

After almost four years of limping through life, I walk the Road of Happy Destiny free, light, and out of pain. The walk of a sober man, who recovered from surgery quickly in the middle of the long, slow recovery others have always wished upon him.

Bill S.
New York, New York

SECTION SIX

Steps to Serenity

I t's particularly satisfying to receive compelling descriptions of the hard-to-describe from our talented members who write in the Grapevine. "My resentments and terror have given way to peace, my fears are being replaced by faith, and my despair is changing to joy," says the author of "Gratitude Was Key." Or, "I applied the ointment of the Twelve Steps to try to bring my emotions to maturity. I became a student, not a teacher. A patient, not a doctor," writes another.

"I work the Steps when I start to hurt," says P.W. from Ohio, formerly a cop-fighting, child-abusing inmate who survived not only divorce but also being disowned by a family who didn't like her sober. Sobriety showed up in her corner.

The author of "What of the Last Half?" describes trying to regain a position of respect, usefulness, security, and happiness in a world from which he had expelled himself. Sometimes emotional sobriety is closely related to common sense, which is most uncommon among active alcoholics, and which can be found in abundance in the Twelve Steps. Another member adds that the Steps offer one of the greatest gifts of all: the ability to stop putting ourselves down, solving the problem of our denying our self-worth.

Then there's this, written by a legally blind member who's just found out that eventually she will live in total blindness: "I've lost my sight, but I've learned to see more. My life is full because my spirit is filled with God. When I feel bad, it's because I allow myself to do so. God waits for me to let him in and lifts me up. So, for those who still struggle with negative 'tapes' playing in their heads, keep on living the Steps and let your Higher Power fill your spirit. The echoes of those words get lighter and lighter—it works, but we have to live it."

Gratitude Turns the Key
April 2010

When I was sober for a few months, I heard that if I did nothing except Step work each morning for a few minutes, that would be OK. So I did, and it was. Now I know that prayer and meditation are the key to relieving the lifelong fear and dread that had consumed me. And they are the key to removing the rest of my character defects.

Gratitude turns the key. By deciding to promptly thank God for any and every situation he brings into my life, I short-circuit my dangerous faulty thinking. Then I can look past the immediate drama right to its acceptance, and sometimes, if God grants me the grace, to its approval—not just in words, but genuinely. If I look for the good and I look inside myself, I will always find something of value in the external situation.

Today I try to look inside first, because I've made the decision to trust God's word and the Promises in the Big Book—not sometimes, but always. I ask that whatever I find that is not a spiritual value, such as selfishness, resentment, or dishonesty, be removed, and I ask for the right thought or action. In this way, God is removing character defects that get in the way of my usefulness to him.

Then I look for the good in any bad situation, and ask that God use it for his purposes, not mine. Either I get a miracle and the situation clears of itself or I find a pesky defect has returned and I'm more ready than ever to work Steps Six and Seven.

In this way, in spite of myself, I have been led to a happy marriage to a kind, loving man who encourages and supports my program of recovery. My once-strained family relationships are now mostly close and joyous, and I've cultivated rich friendships with like-minded people.

My resentments and terror have given way to peace, my fears are being replaced by faith, and my despair is changing to joy.

The Eleventh Step helped me back to the love and trust I had in my youth. But I'm not returning in innocence. I know that life has its heights and its depths and its cycles. That's simply life.

Now I'm secure in knowing that a Higher Power loves and cares for me, always and in all ways.

And now I have faith that no matter what the situation looks like for the moment, there's always some good in it, and that it or I will change for the better if I clearly choose it.

Marie N.
Puerto Vallarta, Mexico

A Bend in Recovery Road
January 1986

When I came through the doors of AA, I had nothing, literally. My three children had been in foster homes and other places because of my inability to care for them. I don't remember fixing meals or buying clothes, and today I don't know how they raised themselves because I was a bar drinker and never home. I had a husband who was in and out of the hospital, and I visited him only because I wanted his workmen's comp checks so I could have money for gas and drinks. I had sold the house when he was in the hospital, and for a while six people lived in a matchbook, two-bedroom house that I rented. I didn't care; I wasn't there. My favorite bar was a block down the road. I became a violent drunk. I would fight with anybody about anything. I abused my children and my husband. In the end, I was fighting cops. After spending a week in jail and really feeling the humiliation of being searched and watched, even in the shower, I was back at the bar the very day I was let out. I never understood. I didn't want to be there. I had a family, I wanted to be home taking care of them, and I could not stay home. Death seemed too good for me. I felt that life was my punishment; I was destined to live because I was such a bad person.

I had trouble when I first came to AA because I thought I was bad trying to be good, instead of sick trying to get better. My recovery was slow because I wouldn't listen, and through my emotional outbursts I was trying to get people to show how much they cared. Today, I know it was because of low self-esteem that I thought no one could love me. Thank God for the people with the patience.

At the age of twenty-seven, when I arrived in AA, I did not have one friend left, not even an acquaintance. I stayed sober my first year because I wanted the approval of the few friends I had made. As one catastrophe after another hit my life in a period of eight months, my sobriety changed drastically and my life improved.

First, my husband filed for divorce and custody of the children. He hated me drunk, but it wasn't anything like he hated me sober. I had to go to court, and the very thing that saved my life was being used against me to take the children I had grown to love. My sponsor died a few months later. I hadn't known she was ill, and no one wanted to tell me because they knew how dependent I was on her. So, when she died I was unprepared, and full of loss. My parents disowned me a couple of months later because I just couldn't do what they wanted me to. They didn't want their daughter going to "those meetings." Never mind that I hadn't been in a fight, jail, or any trouble since coming into the Fellowship. They wanted me to move home and live happily ever after with them; as long as they ran my life, we would all be fine. A month after that, the man I had started seeing (and had transferred most of my dependency onto) said he had enough and wanted to date other women. I fixed that by trying to beat the hell out of him. And I was still sober. I hit an emotional bottom, and in sheer pain and desperation I surrendered to God as I understood him. Period. My dependent self had finally found someone to love and take care of me, and he wouldn't die or leave me alone. For the first time in my life, I felt secure.

Where am I now? I use the Third Step prayer every morning. I work the Steps when I start to hurt. I love to tell people what AA has brought to me, on the inside and on the outside: friends—true, close friends.

My children are with me and we are getting better together. My parents still aren't speaking to me, but I believe in God's time, in his way, it will be okay. The man I loved and cared about in the only way I knew has asked me to marry him. I love and care about him in a totally different way today. I can depend on him, but am not dependent on him. I have recently moved out of a low-income housing development to a real trailer (it was my sponsor's; don't tell me God doesn't love me). The coffeepot is always on for other people like me who are walking the road to recovery.

P. W.
Ashtabula, Ohio

What of the Last Half?

October 1949

Frank stormed out of his client's office snarling, "That stupid, stubborn so-and-so ..." and slammed the door viciously behind him. The jarring impact of the banging door instantly acted as a red signal. Hastily he reopened the door and said to the little man, scowling and scrambling papers on his desk, "Pardon me for slamming the door."

The man glared vacantly, Frank nodded and passed quietly out into the hall and on his way. The dispute that had been raging for three hours had not been settled. An important business relationship teetered in the balance. But Frank got back to his office without a drink.

Nor did he write the scathing letter he had intended to write when he slammed his client's door. He waited until the following day when his sense of humor had returned, and with it some semblance of serenity, patience and tolerance, honesty and self-valuation, positive thinking and a bit of humility. When he finished dictating the rather lengthy letter, he leaned back in his chair and moved his lips inaudibly, "Thy will be done."

It's not important really whether or not Frank retained that account. But it is important to note that he had accepted the fact that he is an alcoholic, and as such it is necessary to safeguard his precious sobriety by sincerely attempting to "practice these principles" in all his daily affairs.

Evidence of this character change might be observed in Frank's attitude toward his landlord who had refused to redecorate, or in his whistle as the elevator man kept him waiting on the 17th floor, in his comments regarding the editor of his favorite newspaper with whose policies he didn't agree, or in his reaction toward his wife who suggested that he forego his fishing trip this weekend and take the family to visit the inlaws.

Frank's fresh attitude in relation to seemingly inconsequential matters or tremendously serious affairs had on occasions been misinterpreted. "This 'Easy Does It' stuff and 'First Things First' philosophy is all right," growled Frank's boss one day, "but don't you think he's carrying it too far?"

Frank didn't believe so, because he was working a desperately serious program—a program of recovery. He was trying to regain a position of respect, usefulness, security, and happiness in a world from which he had expelled himself. And if his program indicated a moment or two of meditation during a heated conference, or even for a missed bus, he realized that his new attitude toward his fellow man would be reflected in continued sobriety.

But sobriety for Frank is now not enough. He has learned that there is a greater and vastly more important victory to be won, that of living with his fellow man unselfishly, with tolerance and understanding. He knows that discretion in the use of tolerance is necessary if he is to continue practicing these principles in all his affairs. For there are times when he has to make a decision between good and bad, and he has discovered that there was just as much harm in being tolerant of wrong thinking and acting as there was in being intolerant of right action.

"That is what is known as common sense," said Frank, "and is one of the essentials in practicing all of the Twelve Steps."

What are these "principles" with which Frank is so concerned in practicing? This is his manner of itemizing them: After acknowledging one's sickness as alcoholism and deciding to do something about it, a study of moral defects of character is made; these are admitted to oneself, God, and another human being; then the realization is made that great physical, mental, and spiritual injury has been inflicted upon oneself and others; but willingness to make amends is expressed and sanity, happiness, and constructive living are achieved through an improved conscious contact with God.

Then these experiences are shared with others, and one practices these principles in all his affairs. Frank believes this can be identified as a spiritual experience, and he is living the AA program up to the hilt.

To keep these principles in action every day, in every contact he makes, would rate Frank a seat somewhere between Gabriel and God. But the fact that he continues to reach for this exalted altitude proves he's making progress in his new way of life. Because in his changed attitude toward his fellow man, Frank has enlarged his spiritual concepts to include a sincere willingness to "practice these principles in all his affairs."

R.G.M.
New York, New York

Confessions of a Reluctant Newcomer

March 2003 (Excerpt)

After treatment, I became, for the second time, a newcomer to AA. A little more desperate than I had been during my first "visit," I made a little more effort to, as Eddie B. said, join the group. In time, I made the shocking discovery that I had little to offer anyone in AA. I knew a lot about books, philosophy, and politics, but nothing about staying or living sober. And until I acquired a degree of humility and became a student, not a teacher; a patient, not a doctor, I would remain ignorant. Intellectually astute (though not as astute as I thought), I was, and sometimes still am, an emotional basket case. I discovered that I was emotionally disturbed, my personality discolored by my reactions to the things that happened to me. I applied the ointment of the Twelve Steps to try to bring my emotions to maturity (and have made progress, but little perfection). No longer a newcomer, I now know through experience that with the help of the Fellowship, the Twelve Steps, and a Higher Power ... I do not have to be a newcomer again.

Wayne B.
Montpelier, Vermont

Step Three: From Sight to Insight
March 2007

Step Three continues to be the most important Step for me. Although the other Steps are important, accepting God and giving up my will makes my life more manageable. I've experienced some bumps along the way, but I have many joys for which I am grateful. If my life were all joy, I'd probably be bored. Challenging times have helped me grow the most. As bad as things may sometimes get, I feel peace inside because I have a history and relationship with my Higher Power, God.

One major challenge has been the loss of my sight. After seventeen surgeries, I've been declared legally blind in my left eye, with half my field of vision. In my right eye I have no vision at all. I never asked, "God, why me?" Instead, I prayed, "God, please be with me and help me get through this." I also asked him not to take all of my sight. It's been quite a journey.

We come to AA to get sober, but within AA we find tools to help us live life. We find a Fellowship that gives love and support. It's up to us what we do with the tools.

Although I've had many growing pains, I've also had far more joy than I ever imagined possible. God loves me and supports me. When I'm weak, he either carries me or, as I've said many times, walks directly behind me, kicking me in the butt to keep me moving. Sometimes I feel like a toddler learning to walk. I take a few steps and fall on my backside. Sometimes I have to sit there for a while. But then I get up and walk again. My legs feel wobbly at times, but the more I do it, the stronger I feel.

Living sober is different from living dry. I choose to turn my will and life over to the care of God today, but God won't hand things to me if I stay in bed and cover my head. I still need to do the legwork. Now, I do things that I never would have dreamed of doing and I see things I've never seen before. I've lost my sight, but I've learned to see more. My life is full because my spirit is filled with God. When I feel bad, it's because I allow myself to do so. God waits for me to let him in and lifts me up. So, for those who still struggle with negative "tapes" playing in their heads, keep on living the Steps and let your Higher Power fill your spirit. The echoes of those words get lighter and lighter—it works, but we have to live it.

I've recently been diagnosed with a disease that will take away my central vision. Since I have no peripheral vision, the impending loss of my central vision is devastating news. It's frightening, but I know I'll be okay. I hate having to accept it, but if I don't, I'm just making my life more difficult. I've cried and will probably do so again.

I'm planning a "scream date" with some AA friends who also have some medical and physical challenges going on. Some people might think we are crazy, but AA taught me to feel my feelings, release them, and then let them go. So, we're going to scream!

Other people ask, "How do you let go and let God? Does it mean throwing caution to the wind?" No, I tell them, but I've learned that worrying about a situation won't change it. I do all that I can and then give the rest to God. And the way I do that is to practice, practice, practice.

For me, the AA program is positive repetition. Each time I live the Steps and allow my Higher Power to help, life is less of a struggle.

Before I came to AA, I knew the meaning of dread. Today, I look at life through the eyes of a child. A leaf, a rock, a handful of dirt, a flower, or a bird is new and exciting. I can't see birds anymore, but I can enjoy their sounds. I can't see the stars, but I know they are there. I can't see snowflakes, but I can feel them on my face.

Although I don't know what tomorrow will bring, I know that there will be AA and I know that there will be God. I may not have a choice in whether I lose my sight or not, but I can choose how to handle it.

Cheryl Lynn F.
Wallkill, New York

Self-Acceptance
June 1975

A lmost everyone I know has, in time, experienced some change in his or her thinking on the Steps. Nothing at all unusual about that. It's part of getting better. But little did I realize how very radical a change was in store for me, particularly with respect to the Fourth through Seventh "inventory" Steps.

Why take a personal inventory? Yesterday, I'd have had to grope for an answer, at least one that I found satisfactory. My uncertainty would have been understandable, since yesterday's point of view was essentially negative. It went something like this:

Step Four—"Stop kidding yourself, Buster. It's time you came to grips with reality. You're really not quite as good a person as you'd have yourself believe. So stop trying to convince yourself you are. Take an honest look at all that's basically wrong in your makeup. While you're at it, consider your assets, too—if you can find any."

Step Five—"I'm impatient, intolerant, and so on. To sum it up, there's a lot that's wrong with me. And the worst of it is, I don't want to believe it."

Step Six—"I've done Four and Five as best I can, so I am entirely ready to have all these defects of character removed. At least, I think I'm ready."

Step Seven—"I'm really not sure why, but I'm awfully uncomfortable. I can't seem to do anything about it. Please, God, take it away."

At the time, I heard it said that the alcoholic doesn't put any value on himself, and I thought: Not so. I couldn't see that the truth of this statement was being demonstrated in my own self-rejection. My thinking had to change before I'd be able to do so. And that's just what happened in another encounter with Steps Four, Five, Six, and Seven. The end result was an entirely different point of view, one that's far more acceptable to me. Here's how I look at these Steps today:

Step Four—"It's time you stopped putting yourself down. Basically, you're a good person. So stop trying to convince yourself otherwise. Take an honest look at the garbage you've been holding on to and recognize it for what it is—garbage, not you. While you're at it, consider all that's right in your makeup, and be grateful for it."

Step Five—"I've been denying my own worth. This is the exact nature of my wrongs."

Step Six—"I'm as ready as I can be today to value myself as a human being. But I can't overcome my negative thinking without God's help."

Step Seven—"Dear God, please help me to see me, to accept and be me."

From negative to positive thinking, but it didn't happen overnight. Getting there took time, effort, and some pain. It was well worth it, though. I finally had my answer to the question "Why take an inventory?" To be able to accept myself once and for all, that's why! As a result, I've little room for the old habit of self-rejection in my life today.

Of course, your own interpretation may be a far cry from either of these. That's fine. It is, after all, an individual program.

The name of the game is using what helps us stay sober today. And while we readily share our views, perhaps one of the nicest things about the AA program is that we don't always have to agree with each other.

Dick C.
Brooklyn, New York

SECTION SEVEN

Finding Our Inner Adult

T he undesirable alcoholic qualities described in the "Twelve and Twelve" might sound familiar to anyone who's been to a nursery school. That famous list may not be welcome news when we're first getting sober, but to those who count on their emotional sobriety to build them a new life, it serves as a warning as we check our attitudes regularly for signs of an inner child tantrum. And we find that evidence much too often.

In another Grapevine book, *Voices of Long-Term Sobriety,* a member writes, "It was there my real adult life began." He was talking about an alcoholic ward in a hospital, where he spent six days at the age of 34 and where one of the visitors to his bedside was Dr. Bob. Most would consider that kind of hospital stay a downer, but because that is where he began to grow up, he blesses it every day.

Bill W. has written that immaturity is the number one symptom of self-obsession. Only an adult can deal with life on life's terms, which is a hallmark of emotional sobriety. It's been also pointed out that the Traditions were written with mature members in mind.

In this chapter is a story from a member who recognizes that his profanity is a measure of his immaturity, and another from a member who recalls his mantra as a newcomer: "They don't know how sensitive I am." And then, with the help of a no-nonsense sponsor, he gets it. "I was not a tragic, noble figure, but ... a self-obsessed middle-aged man who had never grown up."

There are ancillary rewards for such realizations, as well. Old-timers enjoy reminding resistant newcomers of a bonus: Only grown-ups can win "the cash and prizes."

A Measure of Growth

December 1975

My use of profanity tells on me. During my drinking days, the further I sank into drunkenness, the nastier became my language. I've witnessed the same phenomenon in others. It seems to me that the more blunt my adjectives became, the more I was consumed with hate and fear.

It's a matter of degree, I'm sure. A good healthy "God damn it" never hurt anyone under some moment of emotional stress. And I may greet an old friend, especially from my waterfront days, with, "You old s.o.b., how the hell are you?" These terms in their proper context don't seem to bother me. But the blunt four-letter expletives do. D. H. Lawrence opened a Pandora's box with *Lady Chatterley's Lover.* According to one biography about him, when he spent some time aboard ship with a moviemaking crowd, he was shocked at their carrying on and, I presume, at their language.

All the so-called freedom of expression we're said to be enjoying seems but a license to let it all hang out. I'm sure that living should strike some sort of balance, a golden mean. I realize that I have to know about the extremes, because there might come a time to use extreme measures. But to use extreme language on everyday occasions, for me, would show that I still had hate and carping criticism as part of my personality, that I hadn't come very far in our program. I might be dry, but I would have a long way to go to healthy sobriety, to maturity.

If I had to use the blunt four-letter words, it would suggest that I still had a lot of growing up to do, that I might be the college youngster still trying to shake up the old folks. I sometimes wonder where the youngsters think we were in our early years—in a vacuum? The main difference, I suppose, was that during my rebellious period of life, I happened to be in the Navy, and that was before Admiral "Z," when a bread-and-water diet and confinement in the brig were the therapy administered to rebels.

Yes, I had a very nasty mouth in those days, and vestiges remained during my first marriage. It took liberal doses of alcohol to loosen restraints during parties, so that my shadowy Mr. Hyde could come staggering out and hold forth on any subject at hand. On politics, art, or good conduct, the complete, instant authority became manifest with sloshing drink in hand, brooking no argument. It's a wonder we were invited back as often as we were. Perhaps I was on the entertainment calendar. I should have learned to juggle plates or tap-dance instead; either would have caused less wear and tear on the old liver and gray matter.

Therefore, you salty dogs who wish to punctuate with profanity, have at it. But don't look now, because your immaturity might be showing, as well as a limited vocabulary.

Sam M.
Safford, Arizona

How It Feels to Join AA Long Before You Have To
November 1944

It was a lovely spring morning last June, warm and full of promise—a day that fills you with love of life and a desire to live it fully, to accomplish all the things you have dreamed, to work, to love your fellow man. It was the first day of my vacation after a busy year—a vacation eagerly planned for and set aside to do a piece of creative work that was a joy to me. The night before there had been a late party to celebrate the finish of the old and the bright beginning of the new. I was shaky that morning, having celebrated thoroughly, so before I started to shop for my new equipment I decided to have a martini or two before lunch. I awoke at twilight with a bewildered sense of loss.

The lovely day was gone. A shiver of terror went through me and then the slow, steady creep of smothering panic. Something terrible was the matter with me but WHAT? This wasn't the first time this had happened in spite of my best intentions and plans. It had happened with increasing frequency whenever I was released from responsibility. A cold, damp sweat folded around me like a blanket and I was filled with violent nausea. Later I phoned the liquor store. I had to have a drink so I could think this through clearly.

At the end of a week with days beginning and ending in the same way I was reduced to despair and gibbering panic. I couldn't go out in the street, let alone ride in a bus. I was afraid to get in an elevator. I couldn't sit in a movie for fear of screaming out loud. Safe in the apartment the walls started moving in on me. The long vacation yawned ahead like a dark valley of horror. In my despair I doubted if I'd find myself alive at the end of it, let alone well and ready for work. There was no reality but the fight between me and my panic, and the only weapon I knew to fight it with was a drink. I had had psychoanalysis and supposedly should not be suffering this recurrence of panic, but it was worse than in its original form. There was no further help to be sought from that angle. Slowly a thought had begun to focus in my terrified mind. Could the panic have any relationship to my drinking?

I didn't believe it for a moment, but in my despair I couldn't afford to ignore the possibility. If that were all, then everything was simple. I'd just stop drinking and things would straighten out.

I hated to stop drinking, of course, because I actually enjoyed everything about it: the taste, the smell, and the effect that gave me a sense of well-being, gaiety, and courage, for I suffered from an awful shyness and tension with people. Also, liquor had been a daily part of my life for years; helping me through difficulties, being a reward for work well done and a solace when I was depressed. In fact, as I thought about it, liquor was a pretty constant companion in good health and ill, for better or for worse. It went on weekends with me and came home with me. It was waiting for me after work and spent many evenings with me when I should have been following some of my other interests. It frequently went to bed with me and was there in the morning whenever I needed it in the last couple of years. It had lunch with me when it could. It monopolized my vacations because I was carefree. I took it with me where I knew I wouldn't find it. Several times I decided that a temporary vacation would do me good, but I never stayed away more than several days.

Generally, it had been a good companion, reliable and restrained for years, especially when I had work to do. It indulged itself on weekends and at parties and plagued me with hang-overs—some pretty bad ones in the last two years, but it had never interfered with a job or made me sick for more than a holiday or Sunday. It hadn't separated me from my friends or landed me in a hospital. My doctor had never discussed it with me, having no reason to, and my analyst had told me that it was not the factor in my disturbance, though it might be wise not to drink so regularly. But now I made up my mind to stop drinking entirely for the rest of my vacation. To my horror I found I couldn't. The decision to do so seemed to enhance terrifically the desire to drink and all I accomplished was to make of myself a battle ground—one part of me fighting to drink and the other part fighting not to drink. The battle lasted one day and that night I got plastered. The victor rode the field for a week in varying degrees of being slightly tight to being drunk. I never passed out, but I kept trying through the fog to figure out what in hell had broken loose. One side of me was making a souse out of me with all the symptoms, while the other was reeling around helplessly.

Then I remembered reading about AA and hearing that a friend of mine had joined. I phoned and went to see her—not, of course, telling her the whole story, but inquiring about symptoms. She advised attending a meeting, where I behaved like the patient outside the dentist's office who decides he doesn't have a toothache after all. I fought every identification of myself with alcoholism. I had stopped drinking with no effort after the second meeting and for two weeks I attended every meeting with the sole purpose, I recognize now, of proving to myself that I wasn't an alcoholic. But in that time I read the book several times and began to follow the program. I talked with other members, but nowhere could I get what I wanted—a flat, factual statement that I was or was not an alcoholic, in their opinion. It seemed that I had to decide for myself with the wealth of knowledge and experience spread before me at meetings, talks, and in the literature. Then, suddenly, I had to go away for two weeks and I began to drink again with the friends I was visiting. But something had happened to me. Sometimes I think you get this program through the pores by just going to meetings, being with members, and keeping your mind and heart as open as you can. Once you get inside, as my father used to say to us kids: "The Lord has you by the hand!" Something bigger than myself certainly had me by the hand. I stopped drinking with my friends and began the work I had wanted to do—placing my whole problem in the care of the Power greater than myself of which I had heard so much. My mind cleared, an unknown sense of peace quietly took hold of me, and my work went well. I humbly followed the 24 hour plan and asked no questions of myself or IT as to what path I was being lead along or what it signified.

That was two months ago. I returned to AA, so glad to be back and with no inner resistance. Since then I have attended all the meetings that my work permits, have started some Twelfth Step work, and have grown to know many people and to depend upon their help and wisdom when I am frightened, troubled, or depressed. The panic has gone and I have no desire to drink now, though I don't avoid parties and situations where there is drinking. There is a new, fresh interest in my job, an unexpected reserve of material and ideas for it, and an unexpected energy of a different quality—deep, easy, and relaxed. Most important of all is a consciousness of a growing experience with a Power outside myself, which I depend upon and trust and which takes over for me things that are too much for me—more things than my drinking. All this fills me with awe and a profound gratitude to AA for this new and happy life I am living.

Beatrice

Grow Up!
June 1999

My sponsor, Bill, and I were driving south on California's old Interstate 5 in late February of 1970. The bright moonlight reflected on the surface of the mighty Pacific Ocean, and the two-lane highway was practically empty. We were returning from the legendary Laguna Beach Men's Stag meeting, where Bill and I drove faithfully each Monday night. What a gathering of old-timers that meeting was. Thirty or so men, all with twenty years sobriety or more. These were the original pioneers of AA in Southern California, and they were tough men with AA dedication.

It was not the type of meeting that a pompous, over-educated, negative newcomer like myself would choose to attend. It terrified me each week, but I showed up because I was even more terrified of my sponsor. Many evenings these old-timers would lie in the weeds waiting for me (or one of the other newcomers) to whine and snivel about some real—or fancied—difficulty in our lives. Then, like blood-starved sharks, they would rip us apart. With great glee, they would point out to us our selfishness and shallowness. I was more often than not the object of their attack, because I was the primary sniveler and whiner. That night, they had drawn and quartered me.

In the darkness of the car I blurted out, "They don't know how sensitive I am." My sponsor didn't answer, he looked straight ahead. There was, however, a tiny muscle jumping just above his right eye. As the years rolled by, I came to know and recognize this twitch as a signal to me to shut up and smile, but being new and self-obsessed, I decided he hadn't heard and so I repeated, "They just don't know how sensitive I am."

Bill was a great shouter. He could shatter eyeglasses with sheer decibels. But this time, he turned toward me, there in that darkened car, and pushed his sentences through his clenched teeth. He said, "Let's get this straight. You are not sensitive. You are an immature SOB."

My Al-Anon wife calls this kind of episode a Kodak moment—those unforgettable incandescent instances we hold forever clearly in our mind's eye; those golden moments that have snatched life back from the gates of insanity and death for us survivors. I can visualize the car, Bill's eyes, the road, the shining Pacific. Now, many sober years later, I remember that moment, and that night. Because I didn't want a lonely, drunken death, I accepted Bill's premise: I was not a star-crossed, tragic, noble figure, but instead, a self-obsessed middle-aged man who had never grown up.

The dictionary's first definition of immaturity is "not fully grown or developed," and that is the story of my life! For whatever reasons—psychological, social, or spiritual—I never reached a level of maturity that would allow me to live in the world on the world's terms. I was always baffled by the problems of life that other people seemed to solve with impunity. After I discovered the magical properties of booze, I had no need to seek solutions. I had a ready-made solution in a shot glass. And because I was incapable of accepting the "slings and arrows of outrageous fortune," I returned to that shot glass again and again. I had seen myself as tragic rather than pitiful. I had imagined myself abused rather than self-destructive. I had been a victim, not a volunteer.

I didn't sleep that night. At dawn I got up and took a cup of coffee out to the back stairs. As the sun began to push the darkness back, I whispered a muddled prayer to the power of the universe. I asked the power to please help me grow up.

A few nights later, I heard a man speak on the Twelve Steps of AA. Sometime during the course of that night, it came to me that these Steps were provided by a loving Higher Power to help people like me mature.

Now, approaching my twenty-ninth sober year, I remember all those newcomers that I have Twelfth-Stepped, all of those men I have sponsored, all the Fifth Steps I have heard, and I know without a shadow of a doubt that Bill W. was absolutely correct when he stated that self-obsession is the number one defect of character in alcoholics, and I further believe that immaturity is the number one symptom of self-obsessed people.

Bill W. also wrote that if AA fails it will not be because of pressures or problems from outside but rather as a result of failures from within. As my years in the Fellowship have gone by, I have come to one conclusion: if AA fails it will be because too many of us remain immature. The Traditions of AA were written with mature members in mind. They depend upon people who are willing to sacrifice their own comfort and their own selfish ambitions for the good of the group and the good of the newcomer. Immature people have a great deal of trouble suppressing their own selfish impulses for the good of the whole.

We see evidence of this immaturity everywhere. We see it in service positions unfilled. We see it in the small number of groups willing to support AA financially. We see it in the rudeness at meetings. We see it in the sophomoric chanting and counting during AA readings. We see it especially in the increasingly smaller numbers of members available for Twelfth-Step work, and we see it when old-timers refuse to sponsor new people.

My prayer today is that I (and the men I sponsor) continue to grow and mature. I pray that I remember each day that my very life depends on that growth and that the future of AA depends upon my mature actions. I ask the Higher Power for the ability and willingness to accept the First Tradition as a guide to my life.

Cliff R.
Oceanside, California

When I Was 15

September 2010

I'm pregnant." I still ponder the pre-drawn sudden wakefulness that always followed my binges of drinking and blackout craziness. Was its cause a physiological response to the overindulgence of alcohol or was it an emotional and spiritual response to the unseemly acts that took place during my drinking binges?

Whatever the answer, this is the statement that jolted me awake one August morning in 1973 when I was 15 years old. We had moved to Florida from upstate New York five short days prior. I was very distraught about the move from its inception, being forced to leave all that I loved—a grandma, a boyfriend, a girlfriend, the only school I'd ever known, and a hometown full of my growing up—for what my parents thought was paradise.

The day before, my parents and I had set out to have a day at the beach. We ended up in Cocoa Beach, about a two-hour drive north from where we lived. I remember that there was ocean and sun and sand, and all the along the top portion of the beach, there were bars.

I had begun drinking in New York when I was 14, after being rejected from the cheerleading squad in my freshman year of high school. I had suspected all along that I was not good enough, not only for the cheerleading squad, but for life in general, and this event confirmed it. When I began drinking behind the school during the same basketball games that I had hoped to cheer for, I found the magic that alcohol held for me: release from the "not good enoughs." From that point on, alcohol was my Higher Power.

On the beach, I found myself alone after my parents went off to find their own good time. No cell phones existed to keep in touch and I was left to freely explore. I know today that only my Higher Power kept me alive that day. Over the years since this happened, vague and desperate memories have surfaced of the places alcohol took me that day: to a bar with strange men; into the ocean, drunk and swimming with someone I did not know; searching for my bathing suit top in the ocean waves; in a van having sex; and being involved in a car accident on the way home.

I'm pregnant, I thought the next morning. I knew it from deep within my soul. And so it was.

I was in a new state with not one friend in whom to confide. It was one year after the Supreme Court case of Roe vs. Wade had legalized abortion, but long before it was a widely accepted practice, especially in the deep south. In late September 1973, after an agonizing month of isolation with my secret, I told my parents, and terminated my pregnancy.

Those of you who are familiar with the darkness of alcoholism will understand that the serious nature of this event might have looked like one of those "jumping-off points" that the Big Book speaks of, whereby we are faced with the seriousness of our alcoholism and its consequences and make a decision to change. In fact, this was only the beginning of my journey to hell and back. For 15 more years, I drank and damaged myself and others as only an untreated alcoholic can. However, by the grace of God, I married and conceived three children, all planned and deeply loved.

Through it all, I carried with me the shame, sadness, and pain from that day at Cocoa Beach.

One morning in 1989 when I was 30, after a drinking binge, I was jolted awake in much the same way as I had been on that August morning in 1973. This time, though, it was my Higher Power whom I listened to, and as I looked into the blue eyes of my 9-year-old daughter he gave me the words that I heard myself speak: "Mommy drinks too much and she needs to get help in AA."

"OK," she replied and smiled up at me with the assurance that only a 9-year-old can have when placed up against such a challenge.

I called the AA hotline and within half an hour, word spread along the AA airwaves in our little town and a woman called me, took me to my first meeting that evening, and became my sponsor. From the instant I made the call, I felt a great relief and a great power, and I felt like all would be well. I am sober because I was shown by my sponsor how to trust God, clean house, and help others through the program of Alcoholics Anonymous. I have had the spiritual awakening described in Step Twelve, I carry the message to alcoholics who still suffer, and practice the AA principles in all of my affairs—to the best of my ability, one day at a time. If I don't, I return to my baseline of "restless, irritable, and discontent," and we all know where that ultimately leads: to the first drink. And for me, to drink is to die. In February 2010, I celebrated my 21st year of sobriety.

My story could end here, but there is more. In February 2009, my husband (who has an AA recovery story of his own) and I traveled to Florida for a winter vacation. One night while driving back to our hotel from dinner, a sign caught my eye. It said, "Cocoa Beach—15 miles."

My husband knew of that fateful August day in 1973 and later as we sat on our hotel balcony overlooking the dark night ocean, I asked him if he had seen the sign. He had. "Could we go there?" I asked him, not really knowing why, but sensing an urgency to go.

"Of course," was his reply. "When do you want to go?"

We went the very next day. Our plan was to try to find, using only my very vague memory, the area where I had been so many years before. Even though I had dealt with this misadventure in my Fourth Step many years ago, the proximity to the location stirred the remaining demons inside of me as we drove toward the beach. We parked and walked and sure enough we found the same ocean, sun, sand—and bars. We walked without plan or talk. We went inside one bar and asked about its history. Had it always been there? Under the same name? It wasn't quite right.

We walked back out into the sunshine and there, across the sand, I saw it. Actually, I felt it. We went inside this bar and it was the same one from my desperate memories. My husband stood and waited while I walked across the floor toward the bathroom. I let every ounce of my sobriety flood me and shield me and project me across the floor. As I used the bathroom, I imagined myself as that adolescent girl in her bikini in this bar with strangers, drinking underage and alcoholically, so many years before. My beautiful, loving husband was waiting for me and we went back into the sunshine onto the beach.

As sponsors, my husband and I complete the Twelve Steps with new people using the Big Book of Alcoholics Anonymous in the way that we were shown by our sponsors. After completing the Fifth Step, we burn the Fourth Step list to symbolize the end of the old alcoholic thinking and behaviors. It proves quite emotional for those who are ready to change.

In the hotel the night before, I had written a letter to myself about the tragedy that had occurred on the beach so long ago. I now opened it and read it aloud while my husband held my hand. In it, I asked God to help me forgive that young girl and allow her to be free of the pain and sickness that held her captive. I let go of the lingering resentments toward my parents, whom I felt had deserted me that day, and of the others whom I'd allowed to hurt me. And I thanked God for the life of sobriety that has been so freely given to me today if I but work for it. Together, my husband and I knelt and lit the paper afire. We watched it burn to ashes in silence, we recited the Third Step Prayer and the Seventh Step Prayer.

Then we walked hand in hand across the street to the AA meeting that was about to begin.

A.K.R.
Cooperstown, New York

THE TWELVE STEPS

1. We admitted we were powerless over alcohol—that our lives had become unmanageable.

2. Came to believe that a Power greater than ourselves could restore us to sanity.

3. Made a decision to turn our will and our lives over to the care of God as we understood Him.

4. Made a searching and fearless moral inventory of ourselves.

5. Admitted to God, to ourselves, and to another human being the exact nature of our wrongs.

6. Were entirely ready to have God remove all these defects of character.

7. Humbly asked Him to remove our shortcomings.

8. Made a list of all persons we had harmed, and became willing to make amends to them all.

9. Made direct amends to such people wherever possible, except when to do so would injure them or others.

10. Continued to take personal inventory and when we were wrong promptly admitted it.

11. Sought through prayer and meditation to improve our conscious contact with God as we understood Him, praying only for knowledge of His will for us and the power to carry that out.

12. Having had a spiritual awakening as the result of these steps, we tried to carry this message to alcoholics, and to practice these principles in all our affairs.

THE TWELVE TRADITIONS

1. Our common welfare should come first; personal recovery depends upon A.A. unity.

2. For our group purpose there is but one ultimate authority—a loving God as He may express Himself in our group conscience. Our leaders are but trusted servants; they do not govern.

3. The only requirement for A.A. membership is a desire to stop drinking.

4. Each group should be autonomous except in matters affecting other groups or A.A. as a whole.

5. Each group has but one primary purpose—to carry its message to the alcoholic who still suffers.

6. An A.A. group ought never endorse, finance or lend the A.A. name to any related facility or outside enterprise, lest problems of money, property, and prestige divert us from our primary purpose.

7. Every A.A. group ought to be fully self-supporting, declining outside contributions.

8. Alcoholics Anonymous should remain forever nonprofessional, but our service centers may employ special workers.

9. A.A., as such, ought never be organized; but we may create service boards or committees directly responsible to those they serve.

10. Alcoholics Anonymous has no opinion on outside issues; hence the A.A. name ought never be drawn into public controversy.

11. Our public relations policy is based on attraction rather than promotion; we need always maintain personal anonymity at the level of press, radio and films.

12. Anonymity is the spiritual foundation of all our traditions, ever reminding us to place principles before personalities.

Alcoholics Anonymous

AA's program of recovery is fully set forth in its basic text, *Alcoholics Anonymous* (commonly known as the Big Book), now in its Fourth Edition, as well as in *Twelve Steps and Twelve Traditions, Living Sober*, and other books. Information on AA can also be found on AA's website at www.aa.org, or by writing to: Alcoholics Anonymous, Box 459, Grand Central Station, New York, NY 10163. For local resources, check your local telephone directory under "Alcoholics Anonymous." Four pamphlets, "This is A.A.," "Is A.A. For You?," "44 Questions," and "A Newcomer Asks" are also available from AA.

AA Grapevine

AA Grapevine is AA's international monthly journal, published continuously since its first issue in June 1944. The AA pamphlet on AA Grapevine describes its scope and purpose this way: "As an integral part of Alcoholics Anonymous since 1944, the Grapevine publishes articles that reflect the full diversity of experience and thought found within the A.A. Fellowship, as does La Viña, the bimonthly Spanish-language magazine, first published in 1996. No one viewpoint or philosophy dominates their pages, and in determining content, the editorial staff relies on the principles of the Twelve Traditions."

In addition to magazines, AA Grapevine, Inc. also produces books, eBooks, audiobooks, and other items. It also offers a Grapevine Online subscription, which includes: eight to ten new stories monthly, AudioGrapevine (the audio version of the magazine), Grapevine Story Archive (the entire collection of Grapevine articles), and the current issue of Grapevine and La Viña in HTML format. For more information on AA Grapevine, or to subscribe to any of these, please visit the magazine's website at www.aagrapevine.org or write to:

AA Grapevine, Inc.
475 Riverside Drive
New York, NY 10115

Notes: